DIGITAL CRIME

Policing the Cybernation

NEIL BARRETT

KOGAN PAGE

Again, for Diana, Jenny and Vicky

YOURS TO HAVE AND TO HOLD

BUT NOT TO COPY

First published 1997

Kogan Page Limited
120 Pentonville Road
London N1 9JN

© Neil Barrett, 1997

British Library Cataloguing in Publication Data
A CIP for this book is available from the British Library.
ISBN 0–7494–2097 9

Typeset by Florencetype Ltd, Stoodleigh, Devon

CONTENTS

FOREWORD

When describing Neil Barrett's first book, *The State of the Cybernation*, it was suggested that writing about the Internet was like trying to shoot a speeding bullet with a bow and arrow. If so, then writing about the future of digital crime is like trying to fly a jumbo jet on two engines whilst blindfolded.

The complex web of the Internet has spawned a new generation of criminals and, inevitably, the need for a sophisticated and swift response from law enforcement bodies throughout the world. Lawyers and law enforcement officials now have to embrace new technologies as well as new rules to govern them in order to keep up with cyber-criminals. *Digital Crime* examines the need for new evidential techniques in crime detection, and looks at the pitfalls which are an inevitable by-product of this new technology: the problems of the worldwide jurisdiction of the Internet; and the need to report evidence of cyber-crime to the authorities in order that efficient law enforcement can be developed. It also looks at the advances in artificial intelligence, the threat of cyber-terrorism and the role of expert systems.

Digital Crime begins by giving an overview of the revolution which has taken place in communication, and the way in which that revolution has been subverted by the criminal underclass to develop almost undetectable methods of planning their criminal operations and of fencing their ill-gotten gains. It then goes on to explain how the growth of encryption and the increase in available processing power has led to a difficulty in cracking the messages of on-line criminals whilst at the same time opening up possibilities of intercepting and hijacking legitimate messages for the purposes of blackmail.

Similarly I expect that the advent of electronic money will result in superhighway robbery on an unprecedented scale, with robbers wearing digital disguises far more effective than any mask which leave no tell-tale fingerprint. Unlimited amounts of untraceable perfect forgeries of electronic currency can be created at the touch of a button and the banks are caught in a catch-22 of extinction if they don't embrace the technology, and bankruptcy if they do and the technology is beaten.

Digital Crime also highlights the threats to high tech targets such as airports, posed by hackers and cyber-terrorists; and the need for properly coordinated and communicated intelligence. The police have begun to embrace digital intelligence methods and this will have a significant impact on solving repetitive crime. Before the millennium, I expect that the computer crime unit or the NCIS successor will be one of the biggest police operations in the country. We – as a Cybernation – will need it.

In my view, one of the most important messages in this book is that, in most cases, there is no requirement to advise a breach of security to the police. Where a duty of confidentiality exists, there is a requirement to advise the client that the breach has occurred. The client is entitled to know and in not advising him or her, you remove his or her ability to determine the risk and to take the appropriate action. By not telling the client, you become liable for the effects of the breach even if it was unforeseeable and best security practise was used. Similarly, where an insecure communications system is used such as e-mail, there is a duty to ensure that the client knows and understands the risk he or she is taking.

Neil Barrett's fascinating, yet terrifying view of the future of digital crime is an essential read for corporate planners, retailers, bankers and everyone involved in security of data and digital assets. In writing it, the author has demonstrated his ability not merely to pilot the aircraft blindfolded but to make a perfect landing. Don't leave your computer on without reading this book!

Nick Lockett, barrister
December 1996

ACKNOWLEDGEMENTS

As always, this work benefited enormously from the help, encouragement and input of very many people, from a wide variety of organisations. I have been fortunate enough to work with, speak alongside or debate issues with experts from very many organisations – far too many to be named individually here. I would, however, like to single out one person in particular: Nick Lockett, barrister. Nick and I have discussed many of the ideas presented here, thrashing out an understanding of the risks and legal position with respect to computerised offences, in particular those like hacking where the computer is at once the 'victim' and the 'perpetrator' of the offence. Nick's input, comments and corrections have been invaluable; as always, however, any errors that remain are now wholly my responsibility.

At my publishers, Kogan Page, first Gabi Facer and then Susan Pollock have been superb – encouraging, bullying and gradually ensuring that the book you now hold is as close to our initial vision as possible. I would also like to thank my patient and long-suffering employers, Bull Information Systems, for their permission to undertake the work – and for the opportunity to explore these themes with ever more customer organisations.

And last – but by no means least – I'd like once again to thank my wife and children for their patient support. Eventually, our study might re-emerge from the piles of notes, clippings and papers, and once again be available as a sewing room! Thank you all.

NKB
November 1996

PREFACE

As computers and telecommunication networks have become a growing aspect of our business and social lives, it should come as no surprise that they are used increasingly to support illegal as well as legitimate activities.

Computers – and especially the Internet – now present the most powerful global set of tools to which our societies have ever had access; a set of tools that support worldwide, near-instant communication – and from this communication, a growing sense of community: a free-standing, rapidly evolving 'Cybernation' that supports and attracts 'citizens' from all walks of life; from housewives to chief executives, from schoolchildren to pensioners; and which therefore also, inevitably, now includes criminals.

The Internet can be used within crimes ranging from 'simple' extortion to the most complicated, transnational effort at money laundering; fraudulent accounts can be recorded in computer files – which can in turn be encrypted, or even hidden on obscure, remote hosts that are overseas and are accessed only periodically; pornographic images can imported in a format that makes them difficult – perhaps even impossible – to detect; computer viruses, credit card swindles, software bootlegging and hacking – these have all become increasingly prevalent aspects within the world of cyberspace.

And this goes further, because as the use of computers and the Internet has spread, businesses and individuals have become increasingly dependent upon digital technology in the broadest sense – and so the theft of valuable components such as memory or processing chips have also become increasingly common.

Despite all of these problems, and the headlines associated with them, there is as yet no well understood and universally accepted mechanism for handling such crimes – in terms of seizing, reading and analysing the contents of an amoral individual's PC or a fraudulent organisation's computer; in terms of preventing such crimes by the careful application of computer, network and other technological security measures; and in terms of using computers to prepare and present evidence in court. Unfortunately these computer crimes will continue to soar, as the use of computers and of global networks such as the Internet becomes ever more common, as individuals seek to purchase goods or services over computer connections, and as ever more organisations become increasingly dependent on their laboriously collected data.

For the police and the courts, the greatest problems associated with digital crimes centre on the difficulties of sourcing *evidence* from computers in such a way as to maintain its usefulness. This 'Computer Forensic' evidence has proved a steadily growing impediment in the prosecution of even the simplest of fraud cases – not only within the UK, but throughout Europe and the US. Largely inexpert investigators find the complex technology and operational difficulties of obtaining computer records as evidence a complicated and convoluted subject; and equally inexpert courts find the presentation of such evidence fraught with potential challenges to its verity.

With a multiplicity of computing 'standards' and data formats, it becomes difficult in the extreme to obtain and process such digital evidence at all – let alone to present it in a convincing manner. However, a suggested protocol for its seizure and handling has been developed in the UK, although it has not yet gained universal acceptance among the many UK investigative organisations.

Progress is also being made in other areas. There have been several successful and well publicised prosecutions of such illegal acts as the dissemination of malicious computer viruses or of paedophiliac material held in a digital form, leading to a growing collection of case law and useful precedent. Unlike the situation in the UK, in the US this progress has gone further still – with the establishment of special purpose investigation and forensic units that have proven to be useful, although they too have not yet established a universally accepted evidence protocol.

And finally, Lord Justice Woolf's recommendations for improvements in the civil judicial system in the UK have encompassed the widespread introduction of computer technology in the preparation and handling of cases of all kinds – recommendations that are mirrored in the criminal courts.

The impact of computers on law enforcement, therefore, goes well beyond the problems associated with the forensic aspect of capturing evidence. Just as computers can be used by businesses and by criminals, they can also be used by the police, the courts and other investigators themselves – to help analyse complicated sequences of fraudulent transactions, or to determine patterns 'hidden' within a mass of complicated evidence. Technology also has a preventative influence – either from sophisticated encryption and protection systems associated with computer networks, or the more mundane aspect of CCTV surveillance in shops, banks and city centres.

Because of this potential for the application of digital technology in law enforcement, there are two reactions to the information age that must be seen not only as invalid, but as outright mistakes. The first is the dismissal of 'new technologies' as irrelevant; new technologies will change the processes of prosecution and investigative work – of all forms – beyond recognition. To dismiss data mining and artificial intelligence techniques, the use of CCTV monitoring or the application of information technology as being 'not true policing' is inexcusable now; it will be incomprehensible by the end of the decade.

The second mistake, however, would be to embrace the digital future in an unquestioning way, welcoming the application of such technology as the panacea for a variety of detection, compliance and forensic problems. Technology can be applied as easily by the criminal and terrorist as it can by the authorities; and very often, the criminal has greater resource, greater skill and (it must be said) a greater desire to profit from that technology than have the authorities themselves.

Beyond these purely *criminal* interests, however, activities such as hacking and other forms of technological vandalism have also found a place within more extreme conflicts. Information warfare – so-called 'Cyberwar' – has grown rapidly in importance and relevance, whether in place of armed, geo-political conflict, or as an adjunct to low intensity terrorism or guerrilla activity. The national dependence on a digital infrastructure within the US, the UK and elsewhere makes such an infrastructure an obvious and legitimate target in the event of open warfare – but this target is also vulnerable in the case of less overt, insidious attacks from within.

Digital warfare can be applied by companies against their competitors, by countries against their enemies, or by protesters against those whom they find offensive. For a judiciary struggling to counter mischievous, malicious or greed-motivated computer crime, the prospect of strategic military or terrorist use of hacking techniques is a frightening one.

We shall see that, on balance, the continued trends towards greater availability and application of digital technology will bring untold benefits. This book is therefore about the *ways* in which these digital technology benefits can be applied – by security experts, detectives and the courts – against criminals. It is not, however, overtly technological; while issues of technology *are* discussed, as far as possible the explanation is aimed at the non-technical reader. This is particularly important where issues of 'hacking', virus writing and related subjects are concerned[1]: this is emphatically not a textbook for the trainee hacker or Cyberwar guerrilla, but rather for those who are interested in a fascinating and fast developing aspect of law enforcement and digital technology.

At least in part, this book is a more detailed 'drill down' into certain aspects of cyberspace identified in an earlier work, 'The State of the Cybernation' [Barrett 1996a]. Where that book concentrated on the social, political and economic issues of the Internet's adoption, this looks at a broader technology range, with a specific focus on the legal aspects (in the US and the UK) – and with an investigation of the way in which relatively harmless hacking attacks can be expected inexorably to develop into the more sinister, dangerous and increasingly hostile activities of Cyberwar.

The book itself is structured around the various aspects of information age crimes, with the technical details provided as a series of Endnotes. Chapter 1 examines the key components of the Information Age, defining the environment of the Cybernation within which crime and detection occurs. In Chapter 2, those crimes which are performed directly *against* these components of the information age (computers, databases, networks, etc) are discussed, showing the ways in which these most obvious crimes have developed in sophistication.

In Chapter 3, this sophistication progresses further still, with consideration of those crimes which are typically performed *using* digital technology – ranging from the storage or dissemination of computer pornography to Internet-enabled fraud and digital money laundering. Chapters 2 and 3 therefore provide a detailed coverage of the criminal aspects of the information age; this presents the challenge to the authorities.

In Chapter 4, we consider the legal and regulatory response to the challenges posed by these new, digitally-enabled crimes. In some cases, existing laws have been strengthened, and in others, entirely new laws been felt to be necessary. Where new laws have been enacted, these have not always been successful – particularly given the way in which our law-makers have struggled to understand the potential risks (and benefits) associated with new technology.

Chapter 5 considers the situation when these laws must be applied in practice. This chapter therefore addresses the issue of using information age technology to support the *detection* or *prevention* of crimes and the pursuit of culprits. Once detected and caught, the judicial process of prosecuting such individuals becomes important. Chapter 5 outlines the issues involved, from the question of digital, computer-sourced evidence, to the computerisation of courts and court procedures.

This, then, is the full range – from crime, through prevention and detection, to prosecution. In Chapter 6, we examine the directions in which this technological, judicial and criminal innovation might progress, as digital *crime* inexorably transmutes into digital *conflict*, with the growing potential of hacking and other information age activities forming part of the commercial and political arenas – and even the battlefields of the future.

Throughout the world, a variety of military, judicial and government organisations are seeking to define and understand the requirements placed upon them by the emergence of a Cybernation – a global community enabled and dependent upon the digital infrastructure of computers, telecommunications and sophisticated software; a community only loosely bound to the real world of geography and existing jurisdictions. In this book, we will examine these requirements and responses. I hope that this work will be seen as a valuable contribution to the policing of this Cybernation – as useful and informative to the professional investigator, security or legal worker, as it is interesting to the lay reader.

1

The Information Age

INTRODUCTION

The late 20th century will surely come to be known as the 'Information Age'. Our companies, institutions, government, education and private lives are enabled and dominated as never before by the now ubiquitous computer, Internet and related developments.[2]

From washing machines to home computers; from engine control units to air traffic management; from weather forecasting to interactive computer games – we are surrounded by digital computer technology with which we cannot avoid interaction. In some cases, this interaction is very apparent: when using an automatic teller machine or buying goods with credit cards, for example, we would naturally expect our transactions to be recorded in some database, analysed and stored for future reference.

In other cases, however, it is not so obvious; even driving through a city involves interaction with road traffic management systems, automated CCTV monitors and road speed analysers.[3] And in some cases, the interaction is effectively hidden from us – such as in the use of telephones or trains, that demand the coordinated activity of very many computerised elements.

Computers and information networks such as the Internet are not, however, the *only* important technologies in the information age: high capacity storage systems based on CD-ROMs; cheap, reliable and portable colour scanners and laser printers; satellite

and fibre-optic telecommunication systems based on the transmission of data packets digitally. All these, and very many more,
advanced technologies are being introduced, along with the
related mathematical, engineering and computer science advances
to allow us to apply the technologies effectively. This encompasses such aspects as the development of expert systems and
other 'artificial intelligence' methods; a growing understanding of
such esoteric concepts as chaos theory, encryption and the application of stochastic or genetic algorithms; and – perhaps most
importantly – a fast-growing public acceptance of such digital
'miracles' as they become ever more affordable, and ever more
essential.

Because of the presence of computers or digital control units
in so many components of modern life a wealth of data can be
collected and analysed by shops, businesses or the police – and
high-speed telecommunication networks allow that data to be
disseminated rapidly around the world. This capability, of course,
brings very many benefits – and equally very many implications.
Most obviously, those organisations have now become not simply
enabled by, but increasingly *dependent upon* their information
resource. We see now business operations – and indeed whole
businesses – that would not be possible without the supporting
infrastructure of digital technology; and that therefore become
increasingly vulnerable to the loss, damage or infection of that
information.

The ability to collect accurate and immediate data about specific
customer purchasing habits, for example, allows retail organisations to perform precise analyses of a customer's preferences. This
in turn allows well targeted retail or direct marketing campaigns.[4]
As competition within the retail sector becomes ever more intense,
an ability to differentiate offers efficiently on the basis of such
accurate preference data becomes essential. Without this ability,
companies would rapidly lose commercial advantages to those
retailers that *could* use this information effectively. In this context,
the collected data is not a luxury but a vital necessity; the data
therefore has a very real, commercial value – possession of the data
itself is every bit as important as possession of physical real estate
or capital goods: information is more than power, it is *wealth*.

This is not only true for retail organisations. Businesses of all sorts, alongside charities, the military, government and non-government organisations, all depend on access to a constantly updated information resource, not merely in order to function better than their competitors, but rather to function at all.

There is, however, nothing new in our need for timely, accurate and comprehensive information. All organisations and individuals have always felt the need to be well informed about their business, customers, competitors or simply the world around them. What *is* new is the sheer volume of information that we can now collect – and the availability of powerful computer resources allowing that information to be analysed and disseminated around the world.

Information also has more than a commercial value. Computerised control units are responsible for the coordination of traffic lights, railway points, airports – and even cars, trains and planes themselves. Computers make our lives easy in a host of ways; they also ensure that our lives are safe, by rapidly and accurately controlling a myriad of everyday elements with a reliability far in excess of that possible by direct human control. In time, artificial intelligence might perhaps replace human judgement – but we can already see digital technology replacing human reaction times.

And finally, this widespread data resource has a value of sorts for the people to whom it refers. Health, salary and banking records are of course sensitive, but equally so too are supermarket spending patterns; or home video choices; or even book, magazine and newspaper purchases. Each of these taken individually might seem entirely free from threat of civil liberties infringement – but when taken together these hundreds of databases contain information that allows the most comprehensive and detailed picture of individuals to be constructed: by police investigators, by direct marketing companies – or by extortionists. Although the data might not have a direct, monetary value for the person involved, they might well be prepared to spend huge sums to protect themselves from exposure – or even to ensure that certain records are changed.

Digital technology, therefore, provides the basic components of the information age, allowing the most comprehensive of data collections to be stored, analysed and acted upon. The information is of value; to the shops and organisations that would like to profit from understanding an individual's preferences, and that have spent vast sums on the data itself or on the means to collect and analyse the data – or to the operators of the equipment, aircraft or rolling stock controlled by the computerised elements.

The computers themselves are of course valuable; but a PC costing a few thousand pounds can easily contain information whose value is many hundreds of thousands, perhaps even millions of pounds. In some cases, the information might be literally invaluable and entirely irreplaceable – life or death might depend on the information remaining accurate and accessible.[5]

In addition to information that has an operational value, the computers and networks that now straddle the globe can store, process or transmit data that represents 'real-world' value directly. Banks, for example, distribute funds by means of computer networks; money is no longer embodied purely in coins and notes, but now in encrypted, compressed binary signals flowing along copper and fibre-optic cables – both within and between countries. Information *is* wealth.

DIGITAL CRIMES

Wealth, however, inevitably attracts theft. Most obviously, the digital signals representing money might be intercepted and stolen. Instead of shotguns and stocking-masks, bank robbers can now use computer networks and sophisticated software utilities – and rather than attacking the banks directly, and in person, they can strike from overseas, perhaps from the other side of the world via telephone or Internet connections. But this goes further than simple theft. A corporate and societal dependence on vulnerable information resources allows crimes ranging from 'hijack', through 'terrorism' to 'vandalism' – all carried out against information [Warren 1996].

As we shall see, databases can be held to ransom following infection by malicious viruses; so-called 'hostile applets' can be delivered over the Internet, denying users access to their own computing resources; well-placed explosives can destroy communication links, with effects as severe as larger scale attacks against whole buildings; or high intensity radio fields can be used – fired from so-called 'HIRF' guns, to destroy stored data and even computing resources with effects similar to a nuclear explosion's electro-magnetic pulse. Where information is depended upon and has value, it becomes a 'legitimate' objective for amoral individuals or organisations.

Beyond the criminal (or at the very least, the mischievous) antics of digital vandals, this activity now has a strategic or even political relevance: the information age touches not only our businesses and our private lives, but also the national infrastructure and economics. If hackers can penetrate computer systems within universities and businesses, then why not banking systems, air traffic control, railway switching systems, television and radio? And this need not be performed merely for fun or in an extortion attempt – it can instead form a key part of a coordinated and well integrated offensive; it can form an element of 'Cyberwar'.

More than this, instead of seeking to damage it, the computer infrastructure and capabilities of the information age can be used by the criminals or terrorists directly – to assist in the laundering of money; to hide illegally imported software or digitised pornography; or even to disseminate carefully framed propaganda and disinformation.

From the perspective of the hacker, thief or terrorist, digital crimes therefore involve using computers to assist in illegal activities, subverting security within computer systems, or using the global Internet or banking networks in an illicit or misleading manner.

And finally, although much of the value of a computer system comes from the information it holds, the physical components themselves can also command criminal attention – in particular, the theft of memory and processor chips from computers, or even from the manufacturing plants themselves, has become widespread. This might not be seen as a 'high-tech' crime to stand alongside hacking and money laundering, but it is nonetheless an important and distinctive feature of the information age – a crime resulting from the Cybernation's dependence upon digital technology.

A major part of these digital crimes revolves now around the use of the global Internet facilities – the communication mechanism from which the community of the Cybernation is evolving. It would be unfair, however, to single out the Internet for specific attention with regard to crime: although it has gained a populist image for pornography and hacker vandalism, it is not the overtly dangerous place it is painted; and much information age crime (telephone phreaking, mobile phone cloning, chip theft) does not necessarily involve the Internet at all. Despite this, the unique and interesting qualities of the Internet – most particularly, the World-Wide Web and the support it provides for global, anonymous interaction – make for a challenging prospect for the authorities throughout the world.

THE INTERNET

Initially, the Internet was used almost exclusively for the distribution of text by a small number of employees of the very many US institutions and organisations dedicated to defence research. Now, however, its use has spread much further. Thousands of organisations offer facilities whereby the growing numbers of householders with home PCs and modems can connect either to private bulletin board[6] or public Internet services (most particularly, the 'World-Wide Web') through agreement with an 'Internet Service Provider' (ISP) such as CompuServe, Demon Internet or many others.

As well as private users, the Internet now also attracts commercial organisations, accessing the services either by means of modems – like the home PC case – or by much higher bandwidth, special leased-lines. Overall, it is estimated that there are now some 40 million users accessing the Internet world-wide – and the numbers are growing so rapidly that it is thought as many as 200 million could be doing so by the end of the decade.[7]

As well as the change in the numbers of users, the *content* of the Internet has changed – from purely text-based electronic mail or bulletin board articles, to graphics, sound and video. This has been achieved firstly by the convergence of computers with telecommunications, and then by the convergence of video technology with these first two, together with reductions in the cost of colour scanners and digital photography.

The Internet contains much that is of interest and of value; it is therefore attracting increasing numbers of people. In turn, as the potential 'audience' increases, growing numbers of companies are choosing to advertise, publish and even trade goods over the computer connections. As the technology develops further still, even more exciting advances can already be predicted: interactive television – in which users download their own choice of viewing – an element of the more general *Information Superhighway* vision; integrated mobile phones and personal digital assistants – allowing access to the Internet and to computer-held information on a permanent basis; video-telephony and even virtual reality environments supporting work, play and other social (even sexual) relationships within the cyberspace medium.

The Internet, however, also has a darker side – in particular, it is widely considered to provide access almost exclusively to pornography. A recent, well-publicised survey suggested that over 80 per cent of the pictures on the Internet were pornographic. While the survey result itself was found to be entirely erroneous,[8] the observation that the Internet can and does contain illicit, objectionable or downright illegal material *is* perfectly valid.

As we shall see, the Internet supports fraudulent traders, terrorist information exchanges, paedophiles, software pirates, computer hackers and many more. As well as the security requirements associated with individual computers, protection therefore becomes more important still in the Internet context. Using global network connections, hacking or system penetration attempts can be made from literally anywhere; login and password security, data transmission security, audit controls and the sensible application of common-sense procedures become not simply wise, but positively *essential* in this environment. The Internet, while it is not the only feature of modern, digital crime, therefore brings the facilities and the threats of the information age closer to home – literally so: home shoppers using the Internet are as likely to be targeted by computer hackers, viruses and fraudsters as are the banks and building societies; and are as likely to be unwitting accomplices to further security breaches, money laundering or undeclared importing.

Most importantly, of course, home shoppers are vulnerable in the provision of credit card or other electronic payment mechanisms over the Internet connections. This means that secure communication and data transmission are positively essential if the Cybernation is to reach its full commercial potential.

PROTECTING COMPUTER SYSTEMS

The information age provides the ability to collect and analyse large quantities of data, and the ability to communicate that data throughout the world by means of the Internet or other global telecommunication systems. This, however, imposes strict requirements on the security of those components and carefully collected databases. Indeed, as Chapter 4 discusses, the UK's Data Protection Act in particular makes such security a *legal* requirement in the case of 'personal' data.

The computers and data must therefore be protected: from accidental or deliberate disclosure; from bank robbers, hackers or even terrorists; from a company's competitors – and even from their employees.

A variety of security controls exist to deliver this protection, from passwords on files held in Psion Organisers, to the most complex, Kerberos-based token system implemented on huge computer networks. The success of any hacking attack or digital crime, however, typically requires this security to be subverted; and perhaps the most successful element of crime prevention is the provision of enhanced security within computer systems – or even in 'real-world' elements by the application of digital technology. Computers can thus secure themselves, and also buildings, lorries, cars and so on.

This becomes, however, a game of 'cat and mouse': the digital crook seeks out that single necessary loophole; and the security administrators try to ensure that every possible hole has been blocked – either in anticipation or as a result of a successful attack.

In most cases, computer security centres on *Access and Authentication Control*: the ability to restrict access to the computer resources through password-protected login procedures that establish and authenticate a user's identity. Simply preventing unauthorised users from getting on to the computer is not, however, sufficient. It is also necessary to provide further access controls on the files of data and programs contained within the system, restricting even authorised users to just those programs and data files for which they have the appropriate permissions.

User names, passwords, permissions and file access controls are a feature of all multi-user computer systems – but as we shall discuss, they can be easily subverted by the determined hacker. Because of this, further security is required, to ensure that the activities of even authorised users can be monitored and, if necessary, reversed should they damage any part of the system (accidentally or deliberately).

This is called *Audit Control*, and includes such elements as command logging and system monitoring. At its simplest, this merely requires the definition of so-called 'security events': activities that can be performed by users, and which have implications for security. For example, when a user first accesses the system, this is a security event; when they execute an administrative command, this too is a security event; and if they should *change* their user identity, this must also be seen as an 'event'. Audit control then involves recording each such event – together with date, time, identity, and so on – in a large 'Audit Log' file that can subsequently be examined in the situation in which security breaches have occurred.

More than this, the audit log can help identify that a security breach has occurred – this is not always straightforward to discover, given that the system might well support several hundred concurrent users, performing literally millions of processing tasks: the audit log can grow very large, very quickly. The most sophisticated such systems therefore also provide search and analysis tools that can be used to assess the contents of the log on a frequent basis.

The final aspect is *Data Security*, which is relevant both for the storage of data in computer memories and for its transmission over network connections. This covers three sub-elements: *data integrity* (ensuring that the data has not been changed); *data encryption* (ensuring that it cannot be understood if it is intercepted or accessed); and *data repudiation* (ensuring that the recipients of the data are known and are unable to deny receipt).

The importance of repudiation can be seen in the context of digital goods – these might be bought and shipped over Internet connections. Data integrity security ensures that the goods are not damaged in transit through 'noisy' network connections; data encryption ensures that no third party can intercept and thereby steal the goods. These two are very straightforward. In repudiation security, however, the seller of the goods must know that the buyer did indeed receive them, at a particular date and time. If the buyer subsequently denies receipt, the repudiation security measures (say, encrypted receipt tokens) can be used to prove the validity of a seller's claims. Similarly, repudiation security can allow the buyer to prove that the seller did indeed receive payment, should the dispute be in the other direction. Again, however, all these elements can be subverted.

SUBVERTING COMPUTER SECURITY

It is a sad truth that computer security acts as much as a challenge for hackers and criminals as it serves as a protection.

Security measures of all sorts have been attacked in a variety of ways – some of them very sophisticated indeed. In the case of encryption, for example, the attacks have been based not upon 'breaking' the code itself – a technically demanding, perhaps even impossible task in most cases – but rather by guessing or deducing the encryption keys used.[9]

Encryption works by the application of a complex series of convolutions applied to the original data – the so-called 'plaintext'. To ensure that the encryption produces different results when used by different people at different times, it is controlled by an encryption key – this is a numeric value, of say 40, 56, 128 or perhaps even more bits, chosen either by the user, or produced automatically through a random number generator.

In 'Symmetric Encryptions', the key that is used to encrypt the message is also then used – reapplied – to decrypt it; the DES ('Data Encryption Standard') is just such a system. Knowing the single key, together with possession of the encrypted material and the algorithm itself, is then sufficient to decrypt the message, recovering the plaintext. If the key is only short (and 40 bit keys *are* short), then it is not impossible to attempt each and every single, possible key in a 'brute force' attack. Alternatively, in the Internet context, it is necessary for the symmetric key to be communicated to the recipient of the message: it is certainly possible to intercept this key transmission, again allowing the messages to be decoded.

To avoid this interception problem, many encryption security systems now use 'Asymmetric Keys', in which the encryption and decryption keys are different – and all but impossible to deduce from one another. These can then be used to implement 'Public/Private Key' mechanisms, in which one of the keys is maintained secretly, and the second is widely publicised. The widely popular 'PGP' scheme uses this method.[10] When a message is received, encrypted with an individual's private key, only their *public* key can decode it; if the application of the widely-known public key recovers a meaningful message (say, a digital signature)[11] then it can only have been sent from the individual.

By using both one's own *private* and a second party's *public* keys, it is possible to establish secure, point-to-point communication between two people. This secure channel can then be used to communicate the symmetric key. Thereafter, the symmetric key algorithm (which is usually very fast) can be used to encrypt the data transmission itself.

This produces a secure communication mechanism – but as we shall see, it is often possible to deduce the value of the symmetric key (by understanding the basis of the random number generator producing it) and thereby decrypt the communication [Davis 1996, infiNity 1996]. Nonetheless, this is a very powerful mechanism, and the exchange of suitably defined certificates is the basis of most protection schemes, such as those involved in repudiation security, where the certificate is time-stamped as a receipt.

These protection mechanisms – passwords, encryption and certificates – are seldom 'free-standing', but rather usually form part of a larger, more useful computer system – a system that must be developed and implemented with a view to providing the required levels of protection. In the context of digital crime, however, the relatively primitive status of software engineering[12] by comparison to what might be considered 'hard' engineering (bridges, roads, etc) means that it is difficult – or rather, in many situations not possible – to *prove* that a given system is secure, or even that it is an accurate implementation of the original, paper design. In the case of secure systems, there is an added complication: not only must they be secure, they must also be developed with a set of applications and users in mind. All computer systems must *do* something; it is not enough for them merely to *be* secure.

This means that even the most secure system is developed with a view to satisfying an end-user, processing requirement within the context of providing security from specifically identified threats – and in the environment of tight deadlines, penalty clauses and so forth associated with *all* system development exercises. Because of these pressures, errors can (and frequently do) occur: within large development teams, errors of understanding, of implementation and of testing can all introduce unforeseen 'features';[13] even the threats themselves might have been only poorly understood or expressed – or they might have changed as the development project proceeded.

Relationships between components that have been developed without adequate integration[14] testing can often be exploited to open security 'cracks'; and when those cracks have been patched (giving an accretion of security measures) the patches themselves inevitably introduce new and unproven dependencies and relationships into the components of the system – as with the 'real-world', the weakest point is often at the edge of a repaired element.

Just as with physical laws in science that cannot be definitively proved true,[15] it is not possible to prove that a system is secure against *all* possible attacks; it is only possible to show that it has remained secure through a number of determined (and essentially *pre*-determined) attacks – or that it has failed in some regard. And even if it passes six months – or even six years – of rigorous security testing, it might well still fail on the following day, or be broken by a hacker who chose a method other than the ones the design team foresaw.

In the context of digital crime (of hackers, viruses and the host of threats we will examine in Chapter 2), it is important to realise that *no* computer system can be made entirely secure; even the US Department of Defense security classifications (the so-called 'Orange Book' classes) demonstrate only that the system satisfies certain specific criteria – not that it is guaranteed to be 100 per cent proof from attack.[16] Thus, the extent of protection might be known, but not the degree of security – or rather, *in*security.

Once developed and installed, even the most secure systems must then be used: they must inevitably allow users to access them, or data to be entered and manipulated; they must operate as part of a wider system – among a set of further processing resources (human or computer) that must be trusted to a greater or lesser extent. This is a network of 'trust relationships', encompassing modules within a computer system, and relationships between computers. All of these aspects of computer use introduce the potential for security breaches – and hence for digital crime of some form.

Systems, therefore, have weaknesses: *intrinsic* security holes, resulting from design or implementation errors; or they might also be used in a weak manner – *extrinsic* security failings. Passwords, for example, might in some cases be an entirely sufficient mechanism – but if users seldom change them, choose simple words that are too short, or (worse) tell others what they are, then security will be breached.

In fact, it is easy to see how password security might be broken. Most obviously, if individuals share or exchange passwords, and change them infrequently if at all, then inevitably a password will become known by an outsider – perhaps through people leaving the organisation, and thereby *becoming* the outsider.[17] However, even if passwords are not shared, they can still be broken. Because the password must be remembered, users often choose passwords that are memorable, such as names, dates, car registration numbers, telephone numbers or similar. These can be guessed if one knows the user well – but even without knowing the user, the password can be determined by a so-called 'dictionary attack'.

In this attack, a long list of common words, names and dates are produced, perhaps with simple variations such as reversal. Other common letter combinations (for example keyboard patterns such as 'qwerty', 'zaqwsx', '1qasw2') can also be added to the list. Because the UNIX password algorithm is in the public domain, it can be used to generate the encrypted form of these words exactly as they would appear in the UNIX password file. This UNIX algorithm is (thought to be) irreversible, but it is easily possible with a few weeks of computing time to produce a full database of encrypted common passwords.

The hacker can then retrieve a UNIX password file (perhaps by logging in as 'guest') and compare entries with the pre-computed list. It is very likely (a near certainty, in fact) that a password would indeed then be found. There are other possible attacks, which will be discussed in later chapters.

However, all of these simple failings can be addressed in well-managed, well-implemented secure systems. The whole operating system cannot be proved secure, but a trusted kernel of it (the so-called 'Trusted Computer Base' or TCB) can be; UNIX file access permissions[18] can be extended to provide very precise access rights to specific, named users – called 'Access Control Lists'; the login and password procedure can be extended by the use of smart cards, bio-metric identifiers [Torbet 1995] and even AI-based question and answer routines; and computers can be protected from Internet hacking attempts by the introduction of 'Firewall' systems.[19]

Despite the potential for even greater protection, systems will continue to be accessed illicitly – in part, because systems are usually not managed with regard to security but rather with regard to easy, open access for legitimate users; and in part because the sophistication of hacking attempts moves rapidly onwards, while the security of installed system remains essentially static.

We might also remark on an important aspect of these crimes and protection requirements. In most cases, computer security is seen as an essential element for those systems that contain particularly sensitive information. Recall, however, the discussion of 'trust relationships' above: we are *all* now part of a global, closely interconnected network of computers, digital systems and personal trust; and the weakest point of that network of relationships can be exploited.

A local system might not necessarily contain sensitive data, but it might be interconnected, via several intermediate systems, or even shared users, to one that does. Weak local security can be exploited to gain access within a target that unwittingly trusts an insecure node of the trust network. For example, a particular user might have the same password on both of the systems. Breaking security on one – allowing the password to be determined – would thereby allow the hacker simple access to the next. Most worrying, the 'secure' system has no way of knowing that such a trust relationship (even a *dependency*) actually exists.

Hackers need not therefore break security at, say, a bank – instead, they might break security at some weaker point. For example, a bank account within a tightly secured system might be difficult to affect directly, but the system that transfers one's salary to the bank might be much weaker; or the salary system might itself trust a further sub-system – say, the company car database – which is even easier to influence. A hacker might not therefore be able to change his bank balance directly, but changing the taxable value of a company car would change his tax liabilities, indirectly producing a higher bank balance.

The trust network means that weak points can be hacked – and are still relied upon by subsequent elements. And wherever systems can be accessed by the unauthorised hacker, digital crimes can and will occur.

Crime against computers

Crime has been a near-universal feature of our societies since the very earliest days. Some of the oldest written records are of laws that indirectly categorise the types of crimes suffered by those societies. By seeking to legislate against amoral or damaging behaviour, the rulers or governments of those societies thereby defined those sins that were thought sufficiently 'important' to merit such attention. Offences against individuals, property or the 'state' – of whatever form – are seen to have been a feature of our human existence for as long as tribes of human individuals have lived together. Throughout the ages, the types of crimes have been essentially similar – although each culture has developed specific laws to encompass those aspects of life that are unique or special to them.

As with other ages, in the 'Information Age' we have, therefore, developed a series of laws that illustrate the central importance of the computer to our modern existence. In the UK, for example, the Computer Misuse Act, the Data Protection Act, and elements of less computer-specific laws – such as the new Defamation Act – help to define 'right' and 'wrong' behaviour in the context of digital capabilities. In the US, both state and federal laws have emerged to control antisocial computer use from 'trespass' to 'unauthorised manipulation'. These laws demonstrate that criminal activity in the information age need not be restricted to simple theft of applications or of components;

a wide variety of illicit activities are possible, from vandalism – in which the ability to use the information resource is damaged, but for no personal gain – to fraudulent trade over computer networks.

In this chapter we will consider criminal activities performed *against* computers: theft, vandalism, etc; in the following chapter, we will consider the use of computers and information networks to *support* or to *enable* criminal activities to be performed more generally.

We might characterise information age crime as being illegal, immoral or antisocial behaviour that is directed either explicitly against computer resources, or that uses computers in an incidental manner, or that could not be possible without the involvement of computers. This is a spectrum or range of activities in which the computer or digital resource is seen to be more and more crucial to the 'success' of the venture.

The individuals involved in such computer crimes similarly fall within a broad spectrum of information technology skills. Some crimes – such as the theft of basic components – need little or no specialist knowledge; anyone able to break into and steal cars, for example, could easily be shown how to extract memory or processor chips from a PC. Other crimes require higher levels of expertise, such as the ability to decrypt protected files or communications.

In many ways, the growing popularity and the decreasing 'fear' of computers acts to support many more such individuals. As ever more people become first familiar with, and then expert in computers – joining the growing Cybernation community – increasing numbers of them will inevitably prove to be crooked. In some cases in fact, it is not necessary for criminals to have specialist knowledge at all: within the Internet it is easily possible to find directions and suggestions for criminal activities, from recipes showing how to create explosives using simple household goods, to step-by-step guides showing how to break security at any one of the Internet-connected sites.

Computer crime can, therefore, cover very many offences. In the context of this book, we are interested in those criminal activities which are in some sense unique to the information age: many crimes involve computers, but in some cases this is simply because the computer has replaced a more 'traditional' mechanism, and the crime itself has changed not at all. Many accountancy frauds, for example, fall into this category: so-called 'inside jobs' that involve a detailed knowledge of the accountancy procedures for tracking and correlating orders, goods, invoice and payments. These procedures can be manipulated to allow payments to be stolen without the records showing the act.

Before computers, such processing was performed using paper records – account books, order chits and so on. In the age of computer resources, these 'books' are stored as computer files, but inside jobs can still occur, involving manipulation of computer records in place of the old-fashioned paper forms. The crime has not changed; there is little or nothing 'special' about such computer frauds – although there is a correspondingly high interest in the computer-specific mechanisms for preventing or detecting such offences, as we shall see below.[20]

In the context of information age crime, however, we will consider a range of offences that *are* 'special' to the dependence upon digital capabilities – from the simple theft of specifically targeted computer components, through the vandalism of computer hackers and virus writers, to the more specialist frauds, blackmail and theft that could be supported within the Internet.

This and the next chapter are not intended to be an exhaustive classification of computer crime, but rather an illustration of the types of activity that are supported and are likely to become ever more prevalent. In these two chapters, we will not consider the attempts to prevent such crimes, such as the establishment of specific computer protection laws or detection procedures; these will be addressed in subsequent chapters. Here, we look simply at what has or might happen in the context of digital, information age offences.

THEFT OF COMPUTER COMPONENTS

The most immediately obvious, headline-grabbing computer crime must surely be the now endemic theft of computer components from poorly protected offices or factories the length and breadth of the country. Gangs, often of professional thieves, break into, or persuade security guards[21] to allow them access to, whole office blocks – most commonly, government departments – or even to the plants in which the computers are manufactured [Lawrence 1996]. They then proceed to sweep through the building, targeting each of the many PCs or departmental systems. In a few short hours, the entire PC population of an office block can be removed or reduced to essentially useless, empty units. Estimates of the cost of such crimes vary extensively, but all stand in the many tens of millions of pounds – some in fact put the total cost as high as £1 billion.[22]

On the face of it, the stealing of computer components might be thought of as a simple example of the more general criminal inclination towards theft, directed as readily against computers as against other valuable items – video recorders, televisions or cars; as such, the crime might not be considered 'special' to the information age as outlined above. In fact, the theft of computer components is a more special crime than might at first be apparent, depending as it does on certain unique aspects of computer technology and the vagaries of the computer industry – and targeted against the very foundations of the Cybernation community, the basic components of the computer communication elements.

The first point to recognise is that the theft is directed against the *components* rather than against the complete unit. When a thief steals a video recorder, for example, they remove the complete unit; it is the whole that has value, not simply the motor or the playback unit. In the most recent spates of computer theft, however, organised gangs have stripped whole offices not of the complete computer units – keyboard, screen *et al* – but rather of just a handful of the most essential components. The usual choices are the memory or the processor chips. To understand why these elements have value to the thief, it is necessary first to understand a little about how the computers themselves work.

A computer program has two main elements: *instructions* and *data*. Both of these are represented by binary 'words' of a fixed number of digits, stored in computer memories. The instructions and data are retrieved from the memory by the computer's central processing unit (the processor) and then operated upon. Firstly, the nature of the processing unit is vital to the performance of the computer – how many instructions can it retrieve and execute in a given period of time? Secondly, the size of the computer memory is important – how many instructions and how much data can it hold?

If the computer has only a small amount of memory available, however, this does not mean that it is limited in the size of programs or of data it can hold. Instead, the computer's disk drive is usually used to provide a so-called 'Virtual Memory'; clever operating system software allows a large part of the *external* disk memory to be used exactly as though it were *internal* computer memory locations. As the processor retrieves data or instructions from memory in response to its program, the data held on disk is copied into the main memory – this is called 'swapping'. This 'fools' the processor – and hence the program – into believing that more memory is available than there actually is. Of course, the disk access is much slower than access directly to the computer's memory; there is therefore a performance cost associated with this clever technique. The computer *can* hold the larger programs, but it cannot execute them particularly quickly. Larger computer memories, however, reduce the need for such swapping between disk and memory – in turn improving the computer's performance.

The processor and the memory characteristics, therefore, determine the overall performance of a particular computer, in exactly the same way that the engine capacity and number of cylinders determine a car's performance. Improvements can be achieved in computers by two very simple steps: the amount of memory can be increased by the addition of further memory modules; or the processor can be replaced by one which works faster.

These are called 'Upgrades' and are a fundamental part of the computer world. Manufacturers, in fact, assume that buyers will choose slow processors and small memories – that is, *cheaper* computers – with the intention of gradually improving the computer's specification as more and better components are made available, or as they find they can afford better equipment; or more strictly, as they find they cannot live with the relatively poor computer performance. Because of this assumption, the computers themselves – this includes PCs as well as larger systems – are constructed so as to make it as easy as possible for the owners or operators to remove the processor and memory components, exchanging them as required. As well as these, owners can improve the disk drives, modems, screens and most other elements as desired.

To return to our car analogy, it is as though the cars were designed, built and sold on the assumption that drivers would in time add more cylinders or larger engines so as to improve the car's performance as necessary – or add better seats, braking systems and so forth.

This feature of the computer industry, however, has two implications in the context of crime: firstly, it makes it easy for the thief to remove the components; and secondly, it provides the thief with a market for those very same stolen items – a market, indeed, that *expects* to be sold the basic components and is unlikely therefore to be overly suspicious when individual components are offered for sale.

Rather than steal a whole PC or even a small departmental system, thieves can therefore steal just those components for which there is a ready market. They could of course steal whole computers, 'breaking' them to retrieve the components of interest. However, the chips are very small, very light and can be easily concealed, so that one thief can carry the components from several dozen computers. By contrast, if the whole unit is stolen then – other than in the case of laptops or smaller computers – it is very difficult even to carry one, let alone a dozen. More than this, a thief with a pocketful of Lego brick-sized processor or memory chips is unlikely to excite the same level of suspicion as one driving a van packed with whole computers.

There are further advantages to stealing the memory and processor chips, rather than other elements of the computer – most obviously, the memory and processors have a high resale or 'fence' value. In discussion of theft, the fence value of stolen property is often overlooked, but it is of paramount importance to the thief. Few thieves – certainly not professional ones – steal for their own use; only the most opportunistic theft is performed with a view to keeping the actual stolen property. The most usual case is that the goods are sold to another individual – the 'Fence' – who pays the thief an amount dependent upon the resale value that the goods have for *him*.

Because of the economics of this criminal situation, the 'ordinary' value of the stolen goods – the insurance or replacement cost to the victim, for example – can in most situations be ignored. Jewellery, for instance – particularly that which is easily identifiable – has only low fence value; only a very small percentage of the apparent value will be paid by the Fence. Even stolen money from a bank raid must be sold through a Fence – ie 'laundered' – and is therefore worth much less to the thieves than its face value. By contrast, memory and processor chips provide the thief with a very high return – often as much as 50 per cent of the equivalent shop price, which contrasts with less than 1 per cent for jewellery and around 10 per cent for other electronic goods.

Theft of computer chips, therefore, has several advantages for the thief. The components are easily removed from the more bulky computer units, they are easily transported in high numbers, and there is a ready and profitable market for them. In the case of the more expensive processor chips, current production shortages – in some cases caused by such extraneous events as the Kobe earthquake, for example! – mean that these are worth more to a thief, ounce for ounce, than diamonds, gold and even cocaine. They can be traced only with difficulty and, unlike cocaine or other drugs, the possession of computer chips is neither illegal nor even suspicious in itself. And once sold and installed, the presence of more memory chips or a better processor is not immediately obvious to anyone other than the regular user of the PC.

In many ways, we should be far from surprised that a growing, profitable and illicit trade in such goods has rapidly developed – a 'Black Market' that is driven by conditions that are common to most such environments: a requirement for the goods concerned that cannot easily be satisfied by normal sales or distribution channels – due either to a shortage or to high prices, or both as reduced availability allows a price premium to be placed on those goods that *are* available.

In the case of computer memory and processor chips, as mentioned above various manufacturing problems have led in recent years to a shortage and thence to artificially high prices. Set against this, recent developments in PC operating systems (eg Windows 95) and in games and application software have placed ever greater demands on the processor and memory configuration of PCs. It is this combination of factors that has led to the support of a black market, satisfied by thieves rewarded by the equally artificially inflated fence values of the stolen components.

This will of course change. The shortage of memory and processor chips will be gradually eroded, until in time the 'legitimate' market is again able to satisfy most of the legitimate requirement, in turn then depressing the fence value of the components. As this fence value reduces such crime will become less attractive, particularly as the legitimate price of components such as memory chips continues to fall; and other (as yet, unguessable) crimes will become attractive in their turn. These might well be 'computer crimes', or might equally be entirely unrelated.[23] Because such chip theft is essentially a 'professional criminal' activity, they will turn to the best rewarded criminal prospects.

This is not to say that such computer component thefts will entirely cease: they will not – or at least, it is very unlikely that they will. As laptops or other easily portable computers become ever more popular, they will continue to be stolen; and a market for computer chips that are known to be stolen will of course persist. The epidemic proportions of chip theft that have been seen in recent years will, however, reduce as the cost and availability of these components improves.

In addition, of course, a heightened awareness of the risks on the part of businesses and other organisations has led to the introduction of appropriate protection mechanisms. Locked boxes or secure rooms to hold systems; fixing devices and chains that secure a PC to a desk; trembler alarms on PC components; even radio tracking to indicate when a component has been moved – all of these provide simple means whereby the theft can be discouraged, prevented or detected.

The theft of computer components is seen, therefore, as the application of 'standard' criminal approaches to the special nature of the computer marketplace and the requirements it places upon vendors and users alike. It is *more* than the simple urge to steal applied to the now ubiquitous computer; it responds in fact to a set of circumstances and opportunities that are peculiar to the computer industry and to the information age. It is, however, the simplest such crime. We turn next to the more complicated, technically demanding crimes – that is, crimes that require high levels of computing skills both to perform, prevent and to detect.

In particular, chip theft and broader computer theft is directed against the computer units themselves, directly; these *physical* elements, however, represent only a proportion – in most cases, a very small proportion – of the total value (or effected loss) associated with the computer. The computer contains software, data and carefully collected and analysed information. As we discussed above, these *non*-physical elements might be targeted by criminals seeking to steal, damage or threaten information upon which the organisation is crucially dependent or the individual would like to keep private.

To achieve this, it is necessary for the criminal to gain access and for the security systems associated with the computer to be circumvented: a difficult, challenging – but for the criminal ultimately rewarding exercise.

HACKERS AND DIGITAL VANDALISM

Where the theft of computer chips has grown to become a widespread and widely reported criminal activity, hacking (that is, unauthorised 'logical' rather than physical access) has also been covered in the press. This has suffered from high levels of media 'hype': an almost hysterical litany of threats posed by faceless, criminally motivated computer geniuses spread throughout the world. While it is of course accepted that such unauthorised access does occasionally occur, it is also suggested in the media that the Internet in particular plays host to a veritable army of teenage computer wizards, eager to hack through the defences of systems, ranging from military (as in the film *War Games*) to financial institutions.

Is there any truth in these claims? An examination of the most obvious reports and analyses of computer crimes would lead – erroneously – to the conclusion that there was little or none. In 1995, for example, UK DTI reports [NCC 1996] show that more than half of security breaches came from the inadvertent introduction of computer viruses; only some three per cent of breaches were attributed to external attacks, and in these situations, it is often the case that the external hacker is anyway in possession of 'insider' security information such as default passwords.

These relatively low figures of external hacking, however, are somewhat misleading; most obviously, they correspond only to the *reported* security breaches. To count in this category, the breach must therefore be noticed, and the organisation concerned must then also be prepared to admit to the security lapse. In practice, fearful of embarrassment and loss of user (or within banks, investor) confidence, few 'victims' report these crimes.[24]

A further indicator of the low levels of detecting such hacking attempts comes from an Audit Commission report [Audit 1994] that showed over half of all detected security breaches to have been discovered by accident, with only two per cent discovered as a result of positive action on the part of security staff. A recent Pentagon report painted an equally dark picture: a staggering 96 per cent of security breaches were found to have been undetected.

What hacking does occur is therefore only occasionally detected,[25] and only occasionally reported. It is likely (indeed, almost inevitable) that much more hacking activity is being undertaken. A possible indication of this comes from the large number and frequency of security 'alerts' issued by organisations such as CERT and COAST. These are computer emergency response teams, organised primarily within the US universities and military communities, that record and advise on hacking and other security lapses surrounding computers.[26] Among the services they provide is a comprehensive and frequently updated list of UNIX and Internet security breaches, together with a means of repairing those 'holes'. Once a repair has been developed (but not before) they also provide details on how the initial security breach was opened. In very many of these cases, the means to open the breach are far from simple – often involving precisely timed generation of very carefully framed instructions.

It is conceivable, but highly unlikely, that the CERT-reported breaches result from careless stumbling on the part of innocent users: most of the breaches require very expert, involved and patient analysis on the part of the perpetrators; that is, they require a determined and premeditated hacking attempt. It is undeniable that the majority of the reported breaches result from accidents or from virus attacks; but the activity that results in much of the CERT advisories cannot but be intentional – nobody simply stumbles over security holes such as the Sequence Attack (described below) or the Kerberos token weakness.[27]

That said, the hacking need not be undertaken from remote, anonymous sites. In most cases, as mentioned above, what hacking that does occur is enabled by some form of 'insider' knowledge: of particular users' login names and even passwords;[28] or of widely known security loopholes and bugs that have not yet been addressed and repaired within the organisation targeted. And even in these cases, the ability of the hacker then to carry out more offensive actions undetected is hampered by the audit and monitor software that all computer operating systems supply.[29] Of course, truly skilled hackers (and there *are* a large number of such experts) can subvert not only security, but also the monitoring routines; for this reason, hacking is an activity (that is, a crime) that should not be ignored.[30]

In this section we will look at the emergence of hacking as a threat, and at the types of attack that can be launched now – and that may be seen in the future.

The emergence of hacking

Computer systems have been penetrated illicitly by unauthorised users – or those with insufficient authorisation – since the very earliest days of multi-user operating systems, often accidentally, but occasionally with criminal motivation.[31] The growth of 'hacking' as a recognisable (and media-celebrated) sub-culture can be traced back, however, to the growth in Computer Science courses in the late 1970s/early 1980s – but most especially, to the widespread popularity of one operating system in particular: UNIX.

Developed at Bell Laboratories (a part of AT&T) in the early 1970s, UNIX, along with its source code, was distributed freely to universities throughout the US and Europe. Running on relatively inexpensive mini-computers, it was for many students their first exposure to the world of operating systems: in particular, operating systems with which they could play and investigate at first hand while the systems were being used as the main computer for the academic department itself.

The students were therefore being taught and were learning about the detailed operation of the very machines on which their own, their friends' and teachers' information and programs were stored. Although restricted to their own file space, these students were all too aware that adjacent, inaccessible files or machines held interesting material – private letters, exam questions, solutions to the week's programming exercises. They even knew that the files held programs that the system operators alone were allowed – or rather, *able* – to execute; programs that would increase their disk space allocation,[32] allow the removal of an unloved colleague or teacher, or even enable access to the wider world through networks and gateways into other systems.

Inevitably, these students began to hunt around the systems and networks, 'hacking'[33] through a variety of attempts to access unauthorised files or remote sites; curiosity, mischievousness and the inescapable challenge can not be denied. Where earlier computer penetrations were performed either accidentally or for entirely illegal purposes by bank staff or the like, this initial 'hacking' – and indeed the majority of current hacking attempts are performed purely for enjoyment: to demonstrate that it could be done, to gain peer approval, or even to show the authorities that their system is not as secure as they thought.[34]

In Chapter 1, we classified these security weaknesses (exploited by hackers) as falling into two categories: *intrinsic* security failings, in which the system itself has been poorly specified or implemented; and *extrinsic*, in which the security measures are applied in an ineffective manner. These observations are appropriate to *all* systems, not simply computers – but in the case of UNIX security, for example, each of these general development failings can be seen quite clearly. UNIX was never designed to be fully secure; indeed, it was designed to be as 'open' as possible. And in many cases, the users – being students – applied the security measures such as passwords in a very loose manner.[35]

These weaknesses will be seen as a recurrent theme throughout this book, adding to the growing problems of preventing or detecting digitally-supported crimes. In all cases, it is important to realise that the security breach, or more generally, the digital crime occurs primarily through a failure to protect against unauthorised access by users: to a computer system, or to data and programs for which they do not have the appropriate permissions; or to credit details, application software or even credit card numbers that should be protected. Even the chip theft example described above depends on such unauthorised access, in this case to the physical device itself.

Hacking, therefore, involves penetrating computer systems, which of course requires security procedures to be circumvented. The hackers have found a wide range of ways to achieve this. A point must be stressed here, however: in most cases, these attacks are performed for the challenge and the challenge alone. The majority of hackers are not motivated by any sense of criminal imperative, but only by a deep curiosity and a fascination with what they see as the ultimate computer 'game'.[36] This is the case even now, when the Computer Misuse Act and other laws (described in Chapter 4) make such activities illegal – indeed, for some this simply adds 'spice' to the game.

This observation also gives an insight into who these hackers are, and therefore why the hacking occurs. In the main, hackers have been seen either as solitary 'nerds', or as members of a teenage gang either in schools, colleges or universities. Hacking requires high levels of technical skill – although not as high as is commonly believed; more than this, however, it requires high levels of *motivation*. The hacker must spend long hours developing a series of attacks, and exploring network connections around the world in order to discover and penetrate 'interesting' sites.

The majority of hackers (even those within the media-celebrated gangs such as 'Cypherpunk' and 'Legion of Doom') are indeed children, or at least young university students, often motivated more through interaction with machines than through interaction with people. An ability to exercise control over a computer, and to use it to communicate with a wider world of similarly interested individuals, is particularly attractive to young, intelligent but perhaps socially clumsy males. As many studies have shown,[37] the popular image of the hacker is indeed reasonably accurate – perhaps through a case of image-fulfilment on their part.

Beyond this, there are also a large number of more 'thoughtful' hackers who see information as a resource that should never be tied within an organisation; rather, they believe that the information should be free, and freely available. They work to release and publicise this information, convinced that access to the facts is a birthright of all world citizens.[38] It's possible of course to appreciate these sentiments – but without agreeing with them. An organisation might spend huge sums of money to collect and process the data; it is a *property* that they own – just as they might own the equipment within which it is stored. And many hackers cause actual damage that itself costs money.

Should hackers therefore be excused – or worse, admired – as simply childish technophiles exploring their world, or as followers of an alternative philosophy of property? No. In the same way that teenage 'joy riders' are pursued because of the problems and damage they cause (without reference to their driving skills), so too should hackers. They cost a penetrated organisation money and time,[39] and can cause needless damage through careless and uncaring activities. More than this, while the majority are indeed only children, there is still a core of significantly more expert, more mature hackers – even some now employed by the telecom-munication or computer companies as engineers or consultants – who can do much more damage if unleashed on unsuspecting computer systems.

And just like some car theft is motivated by more than simple excitement, some hacking is performed not for the challenge, but for the purposes of vandalism or even of extortion.

Penetrating computer security

Many simple techniques for penetrating computer defences were readily found by the earliest hackers: in the simplest cases by guessing passwords, by manipulating poorly implemented system utilities, or by fooling users into logging in on 'spoof' terminals.[40] And the hackers, with the growth of computer networks (most especially, the Internet), found that they were not alone; a global community of similarly motivated hackers existed in almost all of the universities; and where there were none, home-grown hackers soon emerged as Internet discussion groups began to provide advice.

More than this, particularly in the US there was already a well-established set of individuals and teenage gangs[41] hacking – or rather, as it was called, 'Phreaking' – the telephone system: gener-ating illicit, administrative commands to the thousands of computers that comprised the telephone network, obtaining free telephone calls, or deliberately crashing these computers for the most childish of motivations.

In part, this is made possible by the systems that are respon-sible for managing the telephone systems. Voice, data and switching commands are all transmitted equally along the tele-phone wires; there is no 'special' circuit along which the commands travel – this is called 'in-band' control. In modern networks, the instructions are half tones which cannot be gener-ated naturally by the telephones themselves: these are limited to the digits and two command tones ('#' and '*'). However, there is nothing (other than its illegality) to stop a telephone user attempting to generate these command sequences, if they can discover the special tones used. In the US in the early 1960s, it was discovered that a toy whistle (called a 'phreaker') distributed in breakfast cereals could make the appropriate sounds – and phreaking was born.

To learn the special tones, the phreaker would listen (or 'snoop') the telephone line, duplicating the sequences detected to see what they would do. Gradually, phreaking skills developed, and allowed users to obtain free calls, etc. In the UK, tone dialling was introduced at a later date, with the rotary 'pulse' diallers being more common. Even here, however, it was possible to generate illicit switchboard commands through the careful construction of artificial clicks.

This activity (now tone-dial based in both the US and UK) continues, with many cases of illegal computer access also involving phone manipulation to obtain free calls. The growth in mobile phones has led to even more possibilities, with radio-snoopers able to detect the personal code numbers associated with particular mobile phone transmissions, allowing those mobile phones to be duplicated (or 'cloned') so that calls are assigned to the other number.

It is hoped that digital mobile phones (that support packet transmission and encryption) will alleviate this problem, although hackers, phreakers *et al.* have all shown themselves well capable of subverting even the most sophisticated of protection mechanisms.

These groups of phreakers communicated with one another and shared ideas by means of underground magazines and illicit bulletin boards, which were themselves then moved onto the global Internet as it became ever more accessible. The common point of interest between the hackers and the phreakers lay in the computers themselves: UNIX was developed by an arm of AT&T, and became widespread not only within universities, but also within the constituent companies of AT&T throughout the US and beyond. An ability to break UNIX security therefore also conveyed an ability to break security within the telephone network – and further afield as UNIX became increasingly popular in the commercial arena.

Modern hacking, while it is still primarily mischievous in nature, has progressed in sophistication as the early, obvious security holes have been plugged. Extrinsic weaknesses still, of course, exist on all but the most carefully administered site – indeed, by far the majority of security breaches result from poor operation of security measures by the computer users themselves (or indeed, accidental breaches *by* those very users). Similarly, intrinsic weaknesses still exist – but these are seldom now simple weaknesses in individual components.[42] Instead, hacking via technical loopholes now usually involves exploiting *trust* relationships between individual components or individual computer systems within a network environment.

For example, on Christmas day 1994, one of perhaps the cleverest such attacks was mounted – fortunately on a system that was (quite coincidentally) running particularly detailed audit and monitor programs while its owner, a computer security expert called Tsutomu Shimomura, was on a skiing holiday. This attack – called a 'Sequence Attack' – illustrates the exploitation of trust, along with many of the other important aspects of modern day hacking scenarios.

The attack was launched against two systems that trusted one another: one would happily execute commands (even the most privileged) on behalf of the other, without requiring the additional authentication of an explicit login. The hacker exploited this trust by generating commands that appeared to come over the Internet from one of the partners, while ensuring that the two were unable to communicate directly with one another to confirm the commands; the confirmation was generated artificially by the hacker.[43] The commands themselves, seemingly from the trusted root user, caused the attacked system to allow unrestricted access to the hacker who, it is claimed, then stole sensitive software.

This attack illustrates several important aspects of modern hacking, beyond the obvious issue of the exploitation of trusting systems. It demonstrates, for example, the technical sophistication and imagination shown by the hacker in constructing the attack, which depended on an intimate and detailed understanding of the Internet protocols and the behaviour of the systems.

More than this, however, the sequence attack shows three further, particularly important elements:

1 The anonymity of the hacker, who launched and successfully completed the attack from a system whose security he had previously broken, in an attempt to ensure that he could not be traced[44] – in fact, were it not for the fact that the victim was running such very detailed audit programs (hardly a commonplace within the Internet), both the attack and the attacker would have remained a mystery.
2 Rather than attacking a single component, the attack relied on exploiting weaknesses in the relationship *between* components.
3 The speed of the successful attack, which took only some sixteen seconds!

Defending systems from such attacks, let alone capturing and prosecuting the hackers, would seem to be particularly difficult – an aspect which we will address in the following chapters.

Modern hacking activity is not restricted simply to accessing computer systems or files; the growth of the Internet has introduced the potential for hackers to attack many more, network connected computers; it has also introduced a large variety of network traffic. This traffic flows through the Internet connections as packets of data; at several points within the network (such as the ISP connections themselves) it is possible to intercept or snoop an entire transmission. This allows private electronic mail to be read by inquisitive hackers.

The growth in popularity of the World-Wide Web for trading (discussed below) also, however, supports the possibility of transmitting credit card details. To protect both credit cards and private e-mail, Web browsers now provide sophisticated encryption tools – as discussed in Chapter 1. An obvious interest to the modern-day hacker lies in breaking such encryptions – and here again they have found success.

The encryption methods employed feature long encryption keys, generated randomly by the Web browser for each secure transaction. Once encrypted with the generated key, the contents of the transmission should be effectively protected. The length of the key determines the amount of time an exhaustive attempt at breaking the encryption should take. In the SSL encryption mechanism, the key length is forty bits – long enough to require substantial computing resources to break, but short enough indeed to be broken by brute force attacks.[45]

In SSL, two different kinds of encryption are used. Symmetric keys are used for the bulk of the communication. These allow rapid encryption and equally rapid decryption – and in fact, the same key is used by both parties, hence 'symmetric'. As Chapter 1 described, this key must be passed between the two parties in a secure manner, however, so as to prevent an eavesdropper from capturing the key and then using it to intercept the communication. To prevent this, the symmetric key is encoded with a public/private key encryption that is more secure, but which is costly in terms of computing resources. By using these methods, the costly encryption is used only one time, and thereafter, the quicker and simpler method may be used.

The brute force attack would involve trying each and every possible combination of the secret, symmetric key until the message could be broken. In fact, two US hackers – Goldberg and Wagner, belonging to a group called Cypherpunks – discovered in 1995 that while the code could indeed be broken eventually by brute force, this was not always necessary: in fact, the symmetric key itself, generated by a *pseudo*-random number generator, could be guessed; the symmetric keys were produced by a deterministic procedure based upon the computer's system clock. By knowing this key generation mechanism the hackers succeeded in breaking the code. Although they didn't penetrate the security around the transmission of the symmetric key, they could deduce what it was – and knowing this, they could then use the predicted symmetric key to decrypt the messages themselves.

The solution to this problem for Netscape was to change both the generator and the key length – but in time, even these will be subverted by a sufficiently determined attack. However, US export controls stipulate that strong encryption counts as 'munitions', and cannot therefore be freely exported. The US software development industry has a very strong hold on the global market for security solutions using sophisticated schemes, and this there-fore acts to decrease the possible security levels that Europeans and other non-US citizens and businesses enjoy. Within the US, Netscape can provide huge, 128-bit encryption keys that are essentially proof from attack by brute force methods; in Europe, the key is sufficiently short to be attacked by schoolchildren! As the commercial exploitation of the Internet develops, this situation *must* change.[46]

The future of hacking

As the UNIX system and Internet connections have spread further and wider, this digital vandalism has in turn spread ever further. Firstly, more and more commercial organisations now use the relatively inexpensive UNIX machines. While the security on the systems has been improved manifold over the initial, essentially unsecured versions, UNIX has never enjoyed the high levels of security demonstrable by the more expensive proprietary systems. UNIX machines are now being used, however, for increasingly sensitive purposes, in preference to the proprietary systems.

Secondly, those early teenage and student hackers have them-selves also now moved into the wider world, using the systems they understand so well, but now within companies – and in some cases, perhaps following dismissal or redundancy, moti-vated to exercise their skills *against* those self-same organisations. And thirdly, because UNIX is typically run on smaller, depart-mental scale computers, it is most often administered by staff in their 'spare time'. Largely inexpert administration leads inevit-ably to security loopholes – either through the incorrect imple-mentation of operating system routines, or through a failure to correct those faults that have been identified at other, more closely managed sites.[47]

Finally, the Internet newsgroups began to make sets of instruc-tions – so-called 'Cookbooks' – available, along with sophisticated programs to execute those instructions rapidly and reliably. Simply running the 'Cracking' programs[48] or following the detailed instructions, without any requirement for specialist knowledge, allows *anybody*, be they student, hooligan, criminal or terrorist, to break security at targeted installations.[49] An American defence research project has in fact taken these Internet tools and used them in attacking a variety of their own systems, to assess the tools' effectiveness. The success rate has been found to be over 70 per cent, and where they are successful, only in a handful of cases are the attacks even detected by the administrators; moreover, where successful attacks *are* detected, they are almost never reported [Richardson 1996].

In some cases, the hackers may not even need to obtain access to the system directly – instead, digital vandals can launch so-called 'Denial of Service' attacks: repeated failed attempts to login as particular users will result in those users being locked out;[50] or huge e-mail messages can swamp a user or a computer mailbox – these are called 'E-mail bombs'. Cleverly constructed, 'self-referential' e-mail messages can also be distributed: these appear to be harmless, small messages but when opened they grow rapidly in size, eventually filling a mail system to capacity.

In most cases, however, the hackers are now able to break into seemingly any computer system. This of course allows them wider scope, including an ability to leave not just cheeky or profane messages as in the case of earlier hacking ventures, but instead complex programs called 'Logic Bombs'. These are related to the viruses that we will discuss in the next section; indeed, they can sometimes be delivered by those self-same viruses. The bombs can be written so as to destroy completely, or worse subtly change, the contents of an organisation's computer system. They do not begin this activity, however, until signalled so to do – or if no cancelling signal comes within a given period of time.

While hackers have certainly *threatened* to do this, in most cases the bombs themselves are not planted, only warning messages alerting the organisation to the possibility of such attacks, followed by extortion demands. Planting logic bombs is more usually achieved through viruses or Trojan Horses (discussed in the next section); and if the bomb is to stay there for any length of time, requires detailed knowledge and access to a system so as to allow the audit controls (where they are indeed in place) to be subverted. This has, however, certainly been attempted by employees seeking revenge against an organisation that they suspect might shortly make them redundant.

More successful are attacks that involve encrypting sensitive data, and then offering to sell the decryption key to the organisation concerned. In this case, a successful attack can result in the opportunity to extort quite substantial sums of money – particularly if the encryption can be hidden long enough for any back-up data to be similarly altered.

Such targeted hacking and the planting of delayed bombs allows vandalism therefore to become extortion or blackmail. Organisations have been threatened that a logic bomb has already, or could easily be planted. Huge sums of money have then been demanded – some estimates suggest as much as £500 million paid by financial institutions alone between January 1993 and June 1996 – although such estimates are made difficult by the organisations' reluctance to admit such attacks have occurred, fearful of a loss of public confidence in their security measures. The sum is, therefore, believed to be a massive *under*estimate of the money involved – and some 50 incidents have been reported in the US, Europe and Singapore.

Hacking has therefore moved – at least in the public perception – from being an innocent, if rather irritating, aberration on the part of the young computer 'nerd', to being a definitely criminal activity.

Beyond the purely illegal, however, Chapter 6 discusses how this techno-vandalism can become a part of future warfare, as such attacks become terroristic or political in motivation – as the hacking becomes a *strategic* and not a greed-motivated activity.

COMPUTER INFECTIONS

The frightening progression of hacking, from mischievous nuisance to criminal or terrorist damage is mirrored in the case of computer viruses and related infections. Although these programs *can* be put to legitimate use (we will describe how, shortly) they were developed initially with a definite intention to do damage – damage that has now been defined as criminal with the advent of the UK's Computer Misuse Act and similar laws elsewhere. As the previous section discussed, analyses of reported security breaches show virus attacks as by far the most common problem – from PC networks to larger systems.

In the different types of program, it is possible to see different levels of sophistication applied to each: Trojan Horses; Viruses; Worms; and Hostile Java Applets.

Trojan Horses

In the case of Trojan Horses – and the closely related technique of 'trap doors' – these were arguably the earliest such attacks. In this scheme, a software developer – or even a development team – construct the specified or required program. This might be a simple utility, or a complete suite of interacting routines. Hidden within the complex, interacting instructions, however, a specialised element is added – the trap door.[51] When the program is installed and running, the trap door is available to the developers; depending on the nature of the program, it might then respond to any one of a wide variety of conditions.

For example, in a banking system, the trap door could be activated by a request to open an account for a specific name, and subsequently to divert illicit funds to that account. In a hotel booking suite, it could be activated by a named guest – and again, divert funds or undertake particular actions. The action of the trap door might be, therefore, to act as a delayed logic bomb, or to facilitate theft – or within a Police computer, to remove a specific criminal record, etc. Usually, however, the trap door is designed so as to give a favoured user direct and unconstrained access to a computer system, subverting the normal security mechanisms.

The developers of UNIX once claimed, for example, to have installed just such a trap door into the operating system itself – they hadn't, but used this as an illustration of how easily security breaches can be introduced ([Thompson 1984], recounted in [Garfinkel 1996]). Their example involved a modification to the password program described above, introducing an exception that specifically recognised their user names. If they attempted to log onto any UNIX system, the password trap door was to allow them unconstrained, root-level access *without* checking their passwords against the normal file.

Of course, they argued, one could rewrite and then recompile the password program so as to remove this exception, but to prevent this they had also modified the standard C compiler program. This second modification was to prevent the compiler from omitting the trap door code in the event that it was compiling what it recognised to be the password program. And to ensure that the *compiler* could not be changed, a *third* trap door was introduced to recognise when it was compiling a compiler, and to introduce the second and third trap doors into the new program. To hide all of these trap doors, they then claimed to have removed the relevant lines of code from the compiler and password source programs that were distributed with the operating system itself.

By this combination of code, the designers argued that all subsequent attempts to compile compilers based upon their original – or any subsequent compiler – and any version of the password program would *always* contain their exceptional trap doors. All versions of the UNIX operating system would therefore be compromised, since all subsequent UNIX programs – including later compilers – were compiled using this initial program, or a compiler descended from it. This was, fortunately, just an example, but it served as a very cautionary tale for subsequent system developers, indicating yet again the importance of understanding trust relationships within computer systems.

A trap door is therefore an exceptional case within an otherwise legitimate computer program, allowing specific actions to be performed. In the Trojan Horse, the trap door is taken further still. Here, the sole object of the computer program is to perform some illicit act, but it is 'disguised' as a legitimate program. This disguise might be essentially superficial – the program's name makes it appear to be an accounts program, but it is in reality a logic bomb; or the disguise might be more complete, allowing the program to function correctly until a particular condition is met. There is therefore a degree of overlap between trap doors and Trojan Horses, depending on the 'size' of the door.

There is similar overlap between Trojan Horses and computer viruses. In the case of the Trojan Horse and trap door, these usually form a part of some more substantial development project; they are 'built in' to the system, allowing the programmer an illicit, back entrance to an otherwise secure environment – such as the UNIX example. As such, the program can be thought of as acting under intentional control – it is not acting in an autonomous manner. By contrast, viruses act entirely autonomously – almost as independent life forms!

Computer viruses

At least in part, computer viruses are dependent upon the growing popularity and ubiquity of PCs – and on the associated culture of careless exchange of unprotected diskettes (the analogy with HIV and other sexually transmitted viruses is inescapable). PCs are now a feature of almost every office, and large numbers of classrooms and homes. Part of the appeal of essentially identical systems is the ability to exchange files between the PCs very easily, to allow programs or information to be shared, or to allow users easily and quickly to install new applications. The most common medium for introducing such new files is via a diskette – a small, portable, removable magnetic disk that can contain large numbers of files.

Viruses were first recorded at the University of Delaware in October 1987. Since this first appearance of what was then simply thought of as a 'rogue program', the number of viruses has escalated dramatically – passing 2000 in 1992, and now standing at some 9000 – the basis of a huge, protection industry and one of the greatest concerns for security specialists.

The virus forms a part of a program on an 'infected' disk; the first infection is a deliberate act on the part of the virus writer – subsequent infections are a part of the viral 'life cycle' [Levy 1992]. The virus usually occupies the first few instructions of a particular program; it relies on the user of the soon-to-be infected

PC choosing to execute it – early viruses therefore had appealing names like 'sex.exe' or 'porn.exe'.

When an infected program is executed, the virus is the first series of instructions to be performed. In most cases, the virus's initial action is to copy itself from the diskette onto the PC and 'hide' – within obscure files, the operating system code, the so-called 'boot block' of the disk, or even within unused disk blocks which are subsequently marked as being 'bad', ie damaged and not therefore available for subsequent re-use.

Once the virus has 'jumped' to the PC, it proceeds with the second phase – which is to establish a 'home' on the newly infected system. This it does by a series of actions which are dependent on the weakness of the security associated with PCs. Unlike multi-user systems, on a PC the user is assumed to have global permissions: there is no 'special' privilege analogous with the UNIX root user; *all* users of a PC can perform any system-specific actions. Because of this lack of protection, when the virus runs it can proceed to change significant parts of the PC operating system. In particular, it removes all traces of its execution and presence by modifying the data structures that record and report on active processes.

Even more sophisticated viruses exist only as invisible processes in memory, having deleted and overwritten all files containing them – and subverting all attempts to detect and report their presence. They can even be encrypted, or take advantage of the most sophisticated program compression tricks – such as modifying their own instructions, or changing data values before executing *them* as instructions. Some so-called 'Polymorphic' viruses can even seem to 'evolve' new structures in an attempt to avoid detection, or can even infect the anti-virus software itself. Together with the Worms discussed below, these complicated versions are the greatest source of fear for the military and other security analysts anticipating automated breaches, given how difficult they are to detect in advance.

Once the virus has been copied onto the PC's disk or internal memory, the PC has been infected and the virus can then proceed to perform any one of a number of antisocial pranks: creating endless new processes to clog up the machine; removing files at random; displaying rude messages. The more subtle viruses lie dormant, waiting for a particular condition – the 'Friday the 13th' virus is perhaps the most famous of these, although few would bet against the existence of a several more 'Millennium' viruses, and a rash of virus-related epidemics along with the other, already well publicised computer problems associated with the date change to '00'.[52]

This single infection, however, is not sufficient for truly autonomous viral existence – the virus must then be able to infect subsequent systems, again initially by infecting diskettes. This can be achieved by infecting all executable programs on the PC, or more subtly by modifying the operating system programs responsible for copying files to diskettes, so as to have them introduce the virus code into the new carrier. The virus code is copied into, say, the boot block – or new code can be introduced at the start of an executable program. When that program is run on the new system, the virus continues.

Some new viruses have in fact been developed that do not even need an executable program to be run. These are the 'Prank' or 'Macro' viruses that attach themselves to wordprocessor files. These files contain formatted text – for Microsoft Word – together with instructions for how the file is to be displayed: a macro. The macro instructions are performed by Word when the file is first opened, and these infect the system with – currently – relatively harmless (hence 'Prank') effects.

Of course, once the virus has been activated – or a sufficiently powerful detection mechanism is used – it will become apparent and can be removed. However, this usually requires the computer to be completely 'sanitised': all of the infected programs must be deleted and replaced with clean versions, the programmable ROM contents must be rewritten; the hard disk must be reformatted – destroying all of its contents, including that of the boot block – and a fresh version of the operating system must be reinstalled.

For an individual's home PC this is a great nuisance, but little more; in the case of commercial or government organisations having many thousands of units, the cost of this exercise can be immense.[53]

As well as spreading by means of infected programs on diskette, viruses now also spread through Internet connections. Infected files are downloaded and installed on users' PCs, and then proceed to infect that PC and any files that the user themselves distribute – either by means of diskettes or over the Internet.

In all of these cases, however, the viruses rely on the unfortunate victim executing the infected program, either deliberately or indirectly by means of macros. Programs able to *force* the target machine to execute them – and hence be the agent of their own transmission – would not be so dependent upon gullible or merely ill-informed victims. This is the way that the third category, 'Worms', operates.

Worms

While viruses are normally targeted at simple PCs, Worms are targeted at the larger machines – most usually, various flavours of UNIX – that are connected to the Internet. These programs are similar in many ways to the simpler viruses described above: they act by infecting series of vulnerable computers. They differ, however, in that they rely on independently propagating copies of themselves to subsequent 'hosts', rather than on the actions of unwitting users.

To understand how these Worms travel through the network, we will consider the first such example – the now infamous 'Internet Worm'. This program was written in 1988 by a young American student, Robert Morris,[54] as an intellectual exercise. It is not believed – and certainly Morris has always so claimed – that he had any overtly criminal motive in writing and releasing the Worm. It had, however, a devastating affect on the Internet, causing widespread concern as many UNIX machines failed inexplicably.

The Worm's function was to copy itself from machine to machine, following the Internet connections available on each of the infected hosts. To achieve this, Morris had to face and overcome a series of challenges. Firstly, the Worm had to copy itself from one machine to an adjacent (that is, an Internet-connected) machine. Once the source code had been copied, it was then necessary to compile it on that machine, and then to have it executed.

Running on the remote machine, the Worm would next attempt to propagate itself further afield, until – Morris hoped – *all* UNIX machines connected to the Internet would be running a copy of his program.

How could the Worm program achieve this? In the simplest case, the adjacent machine would 'trust' the machine on which the Worm was running. Within a relatively closed environment, such as a university, it is not unknown for little or nothing in the way of security checks to be established between related machines. Access to one, therefore, implies unconstrained access to its neighbour – just as with the Sequence Attack case described above.

The first infection attempt made by the Worm was therefore simply to try and run a so-called 'remote shell'[55] on that machine. Where this was permitted, the Worm would be provided with direct access exactly as though it was a trusted user of both systems. The remote shell would then be used to instruct the target machine to copy and then compile and execute the Worm.

In the more usual case, this simplest approach was not possible. The Worm therefore had a further series of tactics that it could attempt. Firstly, it had a large file of common passwords that it tried using on the remote systems. If these failed, it then tried a series of automated security attacks, based on known weaknesses in common system utilities that would be exploited by UNIX hackers.[56]

These tricks allowed the Worm to proceed throughout the Internet, infecting each UNIX machine in turn. Once a particular machine had been conquered, the Worm would create a temporary file to act as a marker – in effect, to prevent subsequent infection attempts: when a new Worm reached a previously infected machine, it was simply to be terminated.

Unfortunately, Morris anticipated that the administration staff through the Internet would rapidly detect the Worm, and try to forestall it by artificially creating the marker files themselves. To circumvent this, he introduced a '1 in 7' rule: every seventh time the Worm found a previously established marker file, it was to ignore the file and proceed with its infection regardless. Because of this, the vulnerable machines were all too rapidly not simply infected, but positively *infested* with the Worm, to the point that no other processes could be supported.

The machines began to crash, even though the Internet Worm itself performed no illicit actions beyond the infection and propagation itself. Morris was caught and convicted under the then relatively new US 1986 Computer Fraud and Abuse Act – and fined $10 000, even though his intentions, while not exactly *pure*, had been far from criminal. This particular case is considered further in the context of computer law in Chapter 4.

Now, however, there is a fear that such Worms could prove a serious, perhaps even strategic threat to global information resources. To damage such computers, it is not even necessary for the Worm's attack to succeed – in its attempt to infect a computer, a Worm program will try many thousands of login attempts, each of which requires the computer's attention, just like the offensive hacker attacks described above. While responding to such requests, the computer's performance deteriorates noticeably; at a crucial moment, with perhaps several hundred such attacks performed concurrently, it can easily be seen that an Internet-connected machine may be subverted – even if just for a short time – in what we earlier termed a 'denial of service' attack. And of course, if the attacks succeed, the computer might be damaged more effectively. These are developments in the cyberwarfare tactics mentioned above.

The Worms themselves can in fact be used for a variety of purposes, instead of simply to infest or overload the computers. For example, Worms can introduce viruses; they can steal information to e-mail it back to their authors, or they can be used to partition large programming tasks among a huge number of accessible computers. This last can be useful in breaking encryption codes, or in guessing passwords by exhaustive combinations of characters. Although such exhaustive methods are impractical on single – even ultra-powerful – computers, dividing the task via Worms among several thousand powerful (and, perhaps overnight unused) computers can allow even the most cumbersome and inelegant of algorithms to be performed in realistic time periods. Worms that themselves break security can therefore be used to assist further security attacks.

Worms can be an unpleasant feature of the Internet, forcing their attentions on the unwilling hosts exactly like real-world parasites. They can also, however, be very useful; Worm-like programs (renamed 'Crawlers' or 'agents') are used to trawl throughout the World-Wide Web, gathering information about locally held information – in some cases, even gathering competitive prices for goods like CDs, cameras and so forth.

These use facilities of the Web browsers and associated information servers; moreover, instead of *forcing* their way onto the remote machine, they are provided with access through the Web protocols – in effect, are 'invited' on to the systems. The Internet browsers, however, also provide the potential for new Worm/ Virus attacks, ostensibly to the user's advantage on PCs – previously unthreatened by such 'self-directed' worms. This can happen via the increasingly popular 'Java' programs.

Java and the World-Wide Web

While the Internet provides the basic infrastructure to enable communication between users and remote hosts, it is the software embodied in the World-Wide Web that provides the most interest. Information on the hosts is structured as hypertext, in a format that supports a variety of media – pictures, sound or simple text. These are retrieved by software executed on the user's PC (a 'browser') and displayed. Connections between pages (so-called 'Hyper-links') can then be followed at the push of a button.

Before the development of Java by SUN Microsystems, however, the information within a page was a *static* thing. The pages might be updated on a regular basis, but once updated, their contents were fixed. Java allows the pages to contain active programs in place of the text, allowing pictures to be animated, for example. When a page containing a Java program is retrieved, these commands are copied and executed within the local browser – in effect, creating the page contents 'on the fly'. From the previous discussion, it should be apparent that Java programs are therefore essentially akin to the Worms: code is copied over Internet links, to be executed locally. They differ, however, in that such copying is usually under the user's control – the user can be thought of as having 'invited' the program onto the local PC.

The Java programs (known as 'Applets') were developed to provide additional functionality and power within the Internet.[57] Java is executed locally *within* the browser: the rest of the computer is protected from the effects of the Java program. SUN, in fact, produced a comprehensive list of activities that Java applets were specifically prevented from carrying out. This includes such things as opening or modifying locally held files without the user's permission, running local programs without permission, and executing independently of the browser itself.

It should come as no surprise, however, that applets are in fact already being used for such mischievous ends, showing many of the initial claims to have been premature. So-called 'Hostile Applets' have begun to appear with increasing frequency. The language is very new, and so the 'pranks' are similarly undeveloped. Currently these include nuisance programs that execute endlessly, or interfere with the function of the browser. These range from seemingly unstoppable sound effects, to 'Denial of Service' viruses that work by overloading the browser with an endless series of resource intensive processes; the viruses ensure that the keyboard and PC mouse no longer respond to the user, and that the user's PC is effectively locked preventing its use [LaDue 1996, Dean 1996]. This can be corrected by restarting the browser, but is of course irritating.

Beyond these rather childish pranks, hostile applets have in fact gone much further still. Loopholes have been exploited to allow programs outside of the browser to be initiated and files on the PC or system to be accessed directly; these hostile applets were not publicly released and the loopholes were subsequently closed.[58] Others, however, still exist – including a capability for an applet to *force* the issuing of an e-mail message (with, of course, the virus's chosen text message) purporting to come from the user. Applets can also run as invisible processes (called 'threads') that simply capture information such as user names and passwords that the PC's owner employs, and then e-mail details to the virus's writer. These are called 'Key-Press' viruses, and will be considered in Chapter 6.

Applets have also been used to hijack – without fanfare – users' computational resources to perform programming tasks (such as parts of a segmented decryption exercise, as described in the previous section) on behalf of the virus owner.

By appearing to be well behaved, while performing illicit activities within hidden and unstoppable background threads, the hostile applets can remain undetected indefinitely – although current versions terminate when the browser is closed. It is possible, however, to conceive of more subtle hostile applets that introduce viruses outside of the browser, or that alter the browser to allow the applet to run every time the browser is started. These can be developed by exploiting obscure features of the Java language or run-time environment itself, or – perhaps more likely – by fooling the user into allowing them such privileged access to the system outside the protected browser environment.[59]

Just like the hackers, virus and worm writers before them, the hostile applets issued by such Java hooligans started with simple, relatively harmless devices, before proceeding to more subversive cases. While a lot of activity is currently being performed to locate and close loopholes, the pranks can be expected to continue.

What makes these viruses particularly unwelcome – and potentially more dangerous than their diskette-borne cousins – is that they are introduced onto the local PC in a 'no-fault' manner. The user is interacting with the Internet and Web pages in the 'normal' way; he or she is doing nothing wrong – unlike the diskette case, where programs are loaded and executed without first checking for virus infection, a clear breach of both common sense and common security guidelines.

In the hostile applet case, however, the user has no way of telling in advance that an applet (hostile or benign) is about to be loaded and run – although they can, of course, configure their browsers so as not to run *any* Java code. Assuming, however, that the user has chosen not to limit the browser's functionality in this way, by the time they learn of the Java code's presence it is too late – for good or ill, the applet is running.

To date, these applets have not led to the more damaging or criminal activities associated with the established viruses, but such a development can be easily imagined: applet-generated e-mail ordering goods supposedly on behalf of the user, with those goods diverted to the virus writer; applet logic-bombs, with associated extortion attempts.

At the time of writing, no such severe activities have been reported, although it must surely only be a matter of time before applets are used to support more overtly criminal or terroristic activities. In a later chapter we will describe how they – and other such subversive programming techniques – can and are already being used to support fraud, theft and extortion.

SUMMARY – CRIME AGAINST COMPUTERS

We have seen that computers are valuable resources for organisations, and that this value has several dimensions. Firstly, the basic components themselves have a value, in terms of the replacement costs when PCs, chips or other components are stolen from organisations; and those components themselves have a high resale (or 'fence') value for the criminals concerned, making such thefts particularly attractive.

Secondly, the information on the computers has a value for the organisation – it may have been collected over a long period of time, and be unique to that organisation; or it might be private and personal to an individual who would wish to keep the information secure.

Thirdly, the continued availability of the computer resource might be of value for the organisation – perhaps to the extent that the company concerned is highly dependent on the continued access to the resource. Criminals can therefore benefit by stealing and reselling, or through extortion by denying access to the resource or information – either through the reality or the threat of virus, encryption, worm or hacking attacks.

Virus protection mechanisms are now big business, and there is a growing market for more secure operating systems – but still the progression of both hackers and virus writers seems inexorable. Most virus guard software works by scanning files for infection, looking for recognisable code fragments that it identifies as a specific and known virus. However, new viruses appear almost daily; worse, polymorphic viruses change form rapidly, effectively hiding themselves; but worst still, some viruses have been developed to infect and use the virus scanners themselves!

Prevention of hackers also remains difficult, particularly so because system operators are caught in a difficult choice: they must make their systems as open as possible for their users, while protecting them from intrusion. If the protection mechanisms are cumbersome and awkward, it is highly likely that they will be badly implemented, badly managed and badly used – and therefore an open door to the hacker. The strongest safe in the world is of no use if its door is too cumbersome and is therefore left ajar.

Crime against computers – theft, extortion, criminal damage – is therefore a rich and complex hidden economy, in much the same way that car crime is, for example. With cars, criminal activity can include straightforward theft, perhaps with a view to 'breaking' or resale to order; it can include theft of specific components such as radios, and even the once implausibly popular marque badges.

But the cars can also be *used* in a criminal manner: speeding, 'hit and run', escape from pursuit, hijack and so forth. In roughly analogous ways, so too can the computers themselves.

3

Crime supported
by computers

We have seen in Chapter 2 that the Information age resources – computers, networks, databases and so on – have an *indirect* value for the criminal, who can benefit by stealing or by the extortionate threat of damage to those resources.

Such an illicit economy can only benefit the criminal, however, if it eventually intersects with the *legitimate* economy, allowing the stolen goods to be sold to a gullible (or at least, unconcerned) general public, or encouraging the payment of blackmail demands – and this depends on those stolen or threatened resources having a high direct value for the organisations concerned. Even seemingly pointless digital vandalism is only 'fun' if the damaged information or property is of any value to the owners; harming that which is worthless is doubly futile.

This value – as we have discussed – is determined only slightly by the cost of the computing platforms themselves. To reiterate an earlier point, computing resources can contain or provide access to information whose value can far exceed that of the platforms involved.

As well as having an indirect value for the criminal, however, these computing resources can also bring them significant *direct* value. Just as legitimate organisations can benefit from – and indeed, become crucially dependent upon – the use of information age resources, so too can the criminal. Computers, databases and networks can all be used in support of illegal activities, which can be thought of as falling into one of two categories.

Firstly, the computing resources can be used to support crimes which are 'ordinary' in some sense – that is, the crimes themselves are not information age offences, but rather are simply assisted by access to the database or computer. For example, criminals can access databases illicitly (and as discussed above, now illegally) to extract information that is then used in a 'real world' crime: blackmail following abstraction of medical or criminal records; break-ins to houses belonging to those recorded as being away on holiday.

The intention in these cases is not to damage the information resources; in fact, ideally the criminal would hope to leave no trace of the illicit access. While this does transgress the UK Computer Misuse Act or United States' particular anti-trespass laws discussed in Chapter 4, this is a purely incidental aspect to the crime – like getaway drivers that break speed limits after having robbed a bank.

These ordinary crimes were mentioned in the overview to Chapter 2. From the perspective of this book, their interest lies less in the illegal aspects of perpetrating such crimes, and more in the aspects of *preventing* such crimes by the careful application of computer-supported security mechanisms. More relevant is the second case of using computers in crimes: illegal activities that are dependent upon the presence or use of computers, database or network resources to ensure success.

In these cases, the digital technology can have a greater or lesser involvement: some crimes, for example, might only be possible with the use of computers – such as complex money laundering schemes. In other cases, the digital technology is directly involved, but equally the crime could take place without the computer – such as the book-keeping fraud cases already mentioned.

In this chapter, we will look at those crimes that involve the use of computers, networks or other digital technology to support criminal activities that are directly relevant to the information age. As with Chapter 2, it is not intended to be an exhaustive and detailed discussion of all such offences – the criminal imagination is far too fertile for such an exercise. Instead, we will consider the best known and most commonplace offences, starting with the best known of all – computer pornography.

COMPUTER PORNOGRAPHY

If the theft of computer chips and other important components was the headline-grabbing crime *against* computers, then computer pornography is surely equally newsworthy in the context of using computers to *support* criminal activities. From tabloid prurience and mock outrage at prepubescent interest in 'girlie' CD-ROM images, to the prosecution and imprisonment of paedophiles for the dissemination of obscene, illegal and wholly immoral World-Wide Web pages – computer pornography covers a wide variety of sins and sinners.

But yet, is computer pornography anything more than the simple extension of obscene – or at least, dubious – material from print and video media onto a new, digital form? As with the case of computer chip theft, we will see that it is: computer pornography depends upon a very specific set of computer technology features, although unlike chip theft, it is not influenced by aspects of the computer industry itself.

There are, of course, elements of 'information age pornography' that *are* simple extensions of the earlier, analogue instances: the CD-ROM picture collections, for example, are an obvious development from printed magazines; and hard-core videos clearly evolved from the cinema – or home – films of previous years. In other areas, wholly new aspects of pornography have been supported by new technologies such as sex-chat lines, and even video-telephone services to prostitutes.

In each of these areas, however, there is little that is surprising from a technological perspective. The most interesting aspect of information age pornography is in the use of the Internet to disseminate or access a wide variety of images – still and moving, recorded and live. It is on this that we will therefore concentrate.

It has already been observed that the Internet provides access to a vast quantity of pornographic material; indeed, the bulk of the digitised images available through the World-Wide Web is probably pornographic in nature – photographs scanned from existing (perhaps 'underground') magazine sources in the main, although there are a growing number of mock videos, in which the 'action' is animated from a number of repeated still images. There are also a variety of newsgroups dedicated to sexual themes covering all manner of perversions; there are very many themed Web pages, supporting catalogues of prostitutes and discussion of sexuality, most of it in an obscene or lewd manner; and there are bulletin boards, live 'chat' sessions, and even interactive video services providing access to prostitutes.

Within the UK, US and elsewhere, much of this is not merely offensive – it is positively *illegal*. There are laws relating to the publishing of obscene material, the protection of children, and the regulation of the telecommunications services, all of which can be seen to apply to the Internet's use.[60] Within the UK, for example, the 1959 Obscene Publications Act, the 1988 Criminal Justice Act and the 1978 Protection of Children Act can all be used to prosecute those who store, disseminate or download obscene photographs of sexual acts involving adults, or indecent photographs of children.

The detailed application of these laws – together with the computer-specific extensions introduced by the 1994 Criminal Justice and Public Order Act – will be discussed in Chapter 4, along with the corresponding laws of the US, home to the largest Internet population. In this section, however, we will look instead at *why* and *how* the Internet is used to distribute such material.

Pornography and the Internet

The Internet is a new medium, or rather a relatively new aspect of an established medium. *All* media have been rapidly populated by pornography: explicit photographs of young prostitutes appeared shortly after the introduction of the camera; equally, films and videos were soon employed by the pornographers – as were the various print media before them. Should we therefore be surprised that the Internet has been equally rapidly populated? Perhaps yes.

The Internet is not an 'overnight success'. It was developed and used by universities and researchers long before it gained widespread popularity in the last few years. But yet, even in the early 1980s, it was possible to find and download obscene images, or access sexually explicit newsgroup discussions – long before the invention of the World-Wide Web and easy access to those facilities, and long before the pornographers producing hard core films and magazines could access the Internet, let alone use it to distribute their wares.

There might be several explanations suggested for the use of the Internet in this context. The most simplistic is the unsubtle observation that both the Internet *and* pornography attract solitary, socially maladjusted users who are, almost exclusively, male. However, even if this caricature of Internet users and pornography users was accurate (which it isn't, on both counts), it leaves open the subsidiary questions: are these the *same* solitary misfits? Is there even any overlap between them?

The answer in both cases is probably not – or rather, that a definite, perhaps *causal*, link cannot be established: Internet users do not necessarily become pornography users (although the reverse argument can probably be supported, given the Internet's growing bad reputation).

If this simplistic explanation is unsatisfactory, so too is the *opportunistic* one: the Internet is used for pornography simply because it supports the distribution of such images.

There is, of course, an element of truth in this last; photographs can be easily encoded in a variety of formats for dissemination through the Internet and display on local, colour terminals. However, the picture encoding formats are not an obvious and intrinsic part of the Internet; they were developed specifically to support a perceived requirement to transmit pictures. While some at least of these early pictures were transmitted for the purposes of furthering research work, within the broader Internet newsgroups the formats were popularised because they allowed entertaining images to be distributed.

A recurring theme within computer development is the entertainment motivation: even UNIX itself was written initially to allow its developers to use an idle DEC PDP machine for a computer game! In the Internet's development, these first, newsgroup distributed images were digitally captured photographs covering those subjects of interest to the early Internet and BBS users: Star Trek, Star Wars and other stills from science fiction films or TV series; satellite images of the Earth, Moon, etc; and a wide variety of nudes. The earliest pornography in the Internet appeared, it would therefore seem, long before the earliest pornographers.

We might therefore divide the pornographic content of the Internet into three simple categories. The first is exemplified by this earliest application: 'ordinary' Internet users, interested in relatively harmless, nude photographs, made these available to others through publication in newsgroups or within easily located Web pages. At a time when the Internet access was restricted to an essentially adult population, such publishing might be thought of as a harmless – if idiosyncratic – use of the technology.

For many years, the Internet supported such open activities by the original population. However, as the Internet facilities became available on a commercial basis to a wider population, a second category became increasingly obvious. In this, the technology developed by the first set of users was applied by commercially-motivated organisations to deliver access to pornographic publications on-line.

Digital versions of well-known, real-world titles became a fast growing feature of the Internet as the Web became ever more common. In addition, the hard core material was made available over the Internet, accessible behind virtual 'locked doors' for the payment of money to the pornographers or publishers; indeed, in many ways these publishers have broken the new ground within the Internet in terms of payment services for Internet-hosted publishing.

While these Web sites *do* provide access – albeit only on payment of a fee – to material ranging from soft to hard pornography, they are perhaps less of a worry than the third category: the paedophiliac and other obscene material which ranges from bestiality, through perversions, to more extreme subject matter such as graphic mutilation scenes: material that is well 'beyond the pale'.

The paedophile material on the Internet is not widely publicised. The publishers of such images do so for their own purposes, disseminating the pictures and text among a closed community or 'ring' of like-minded perverts – usually without asking for payment. Where the 'normal' pornographers and the ordinary users employ the Internet technologies in a reasonably obvious and straightforward manner, the truly imaginative application of digital facilities lies firmly with this group.

Before considering the ways in which this technology is abused, it is useful to return to the explanation of why the Internet should have gained such a poor reputation in this regard. Most importantly, we must recognise that, while the general image of the Internet as a source of computer pornography is certainly accurate, the adult or offensive content comes not from simply one, generally available type of obscene publication and one type of pornography user, but rather from the combination of the three types of pornography publication outlined above.

The ordinary users distributed nude photographs over the Internet because it was a part of the open, libertine culture of early, primarily adult Internet use – as much a part as free speech within newsgroups. The commercial pornographers employed the same technology because it was available and easy, and because there was a perceived market for their material – and we must assume, since the Internet publishing of such images persists, that they are making adequate money from their ventures, illustrating that the market really *is* there.

The third category, the paedophiles, are the opportunistic users, relying on the digital technology to hide their material and allow its easy transmission in an untraceable manner. This then gives what might be the most plausible explanation for the Internet's successful use in this context: the ability to hide, or at least to maintain, elements of personal anonymity in the capturing and storage of pornographic material; and the ability to import such images without obvious tracks being left.

The opportunistic *and* the simplistic explanations mentioned above therefore both have an element of truth to them, although the Internet's capacity to support complete anonymity is perhaps the most important aspect.

Internet technology use

Turning now to the technology applied, the greatest interest surely lies in the imaginative use of the Internet facilities to hide the paedophiliac and other outright illegal images within the Web and Internet-connected host systems. In the case of the commercial pornographers, photographic images are scanned and stored within host computers in one of a small number of common formats. These are most usually then included within Web pages, on systems that can be accessed in only a restricted way; this access might be controlled so as only to allow users to read those pages for which they have paid, or for which they are eligible through having joined a club or gained an 'adult verification' certificate (again, through the payment of an annual fee).

By contrast, in the case of the paedophiliac or obscene material, the Internet is used less to publicise the images, and more to provide the facilities for storing and transmitting the data in a format which makes it difficult or impossible to detect; less 'publishing' and more 'hiding' of the material.

This is not to say that the Internet cannot be used more openly by these individuals, to support newsgroup discussions, for example. However, given the illegal nature of their interests, the Internet is more likely to be used as a means of transmitting and storing the offensive images themselves in a clandestine manner – particularly since such open discussions can be (and indeed have been) monitored and acted upon by the police.

The most obvious capability of the Internet – or rather, of the Internet-connected computers – is the support for encryption. Files containing encoded photographs can be encrypted in a variety of manners, using algorithms that cannot easily be broken. These encrypted files can then be transmitted through the Internet, secure from capture by the authorities or those for whom they are not intended. Alternatively, the files can be stored on the user's host machine – again, secure from being inadvertently seen.

Of course, if the authorities can determine the encryption key – by finding a written record of it, by successfully demanding it of the paedophile, or by capturing that key when it is communicated to members of a paedophile ring – then they can easily recover the original, offensive images. More sophisticated encryption methods, involving public and private keys such as are involved in the PGP tool or SET standard for electronic mail or credit card orders,[61] can remove some of these threats – but ultimately, the very existence or transmission of encrypted files can give rise to suspicion – and in some countries, such as France, such encryption is itself actually illegal.

The cleverest of the Internet paedophiles (and of course the hackers, bootleggers and so forth) have therefore turned not simply to encrypting the files, but also to sleight of hand and misdirection in hiding the data in a variety of ways. The most obvious of these involves using somebody else's host computer to store the data. By using the various hacking tricks described in the previous chapter, the paedophile can gain access to a particular machine, and can then hide the files – with non-obvious names – within seldom-used directories. It is even possible to embed the data *within* a legitimate file, rather similar to the way in which viruses are hidden.

More sophisticated yet, the data that constitutes the images can itself be hidden within an innocent image. Several mechanisms have been developed to encode data in the tiny symbols used to generate images in printing. In most cases, pictures are made up of various coloured dots; however, if a range of tiny symbols are used instead (dot, square, triangle, etc) then it becomes possible to encode *any* data within the picture, using the shading and colouring to store it in a clandestine manner.

This ostensibly innocent picture can then be transmitted over the Internet, and the offensive picture abstracted by those knowing to look for it, and knowing the encoding format in use. At the time of writing, this trick has not yet gained widespread use – but it can be expected to become more popular as the algorithms become more widely known.

An even simpler version of this trick involves the background image that many Web pages use. This is a pattern upon which the page's text, pictures and so forth are overlaid; it is, however, simply an ordinary picture file like all the others, but 'tiled' (that is, copied an appropriate number of times) to cover the whole page. It can be used, though, to hold the illicit information.

The binary contents of the illicit file can be used, for example, to give black and white dots; these are then stored as the picture – giving a grey, marble-like effect. It can even be in colour – producing a pretty, innocent looking backcloth over which harmless text is written; but the real, intended contents of the page – in plain view – are within this backcloth. Only those who know where – and indeed, how – to look can then retrieve and decode the intended transmission, be it pictures, text or anything.[62]

Computer systems allow data to be hidden in many other ways yet be in 'plain view'. Sound files, for example, can contain illicit data. Within a file of audible sound, it is possible to encode data as a very high pitch, very low intensity sound channel carrying the 1s and 0s – in effect, an inaudible version of the 'warble' heard from modems. Again, those who know can extract the illicit data without difficulty.[63]

The Web provides yet more opportunities. In particular, if a given host is not publicised by means of the ubiquitous search engines, it will be accessible only to those who know its address. These people can access it directly, or via some other, apparently innocent Web page containing a link. A particularly subtle trick is to provide what appears to be a Web 'dead end': when the user tries to retrieve a non-existent page, a common error message is displayed: 'Error 404'. This means that the page is not present on the machine. Most users, faced with this message, return to their start point and search elsewhere. However, clever hackers and paedophiles can hide links to illicit machines within at least some of these error pages. The pages are easy to duplicate, and the links are placed several screens below the message, to make them as non-obvious as possible. Links can also be grey-on-grey, or even hidden within pages that purport to be genuine. Such misdirection is not immediately obvious to those seeking to detect the paedophile or hacker (see Chapter 5).

Paedophile material can therefore be stored on other peoples' machines, in an encrypted format, or hidden on inaccessible or at least very non-obvious Internet hosts. While all of these clever mechanisms can, and are, used by others to hide illicit company accounts, bootleg software and so forth, their use by paedophiles and other pornographers is the most noteworthy.

The Internet has been described by many as a 'Bad Neighbourhood', or as being a haven for pornography. This is certainly true: the Internet provides very many niches within which such immoral activity can be performed. It also supports criminal activity which is wholly *amoral* in nature.

BOOTLEG SOFTWARE DISTRIBUTION

Where computer pornography results from the 'invasion' of illegally explicit material into a new medium, the features of computer use and the communication potential of the Internet can support more intrinsic crimes. In particular, the central importance of expensive software in the operation of computers of all kinds 'justifies' illegal trade in this digital property. As with the previous examples of crime in the digital context, we will again see that this illegal trade depends on the successful application of key features of the information age: the ubiquitous Internet communication mechanism; the digital nature of the property itself; and the organisation of software within computers.

The motivation for software theft

The most commonly used computers are now PCs – a fast-growing feature of homes, schools and offices throughout the developed world. Apart from the data that they hold – which might, as we have discussed above, have a high value for the individuals or organisations concerned – they also hold typically three types of software program. Firstly, they all contain *operating system* software. This is the set of programs that make the basic computing platform useable; it ensures that the printers, network connections and files are all managed correctly and work effectively. In PCs, this system software includes such well-known items as DOS, Windows or MacOS; or UNIX, VMS *et al* on the larger machines; all computers require operating system software of varying levels of complexity.

In itself, however, this operating system does little more than make the computer potentially useful. It is the second category of software – *applications* – that provides the real value. These applications vary from PC to PC, and from organisation to organisation. General applications include word processing, database and even Internet-access utilities; bespoke applications are those that have been developed specifically for the organisation or individual owning or operating the computer. These applications allow the computer to perform real *work* on behalf the owners.

The final category of software is *games*, which are similar in many ways to applications insofar as they are both 'optional' and both require support from the operating system, providing the computer with its 'personality'. In the case of games, however, these are (obviously) not the work, but rather the recreational aspect of computer use, but are nonetheless important.

Operating system, application and games software are therefore a feature of all PCs – and indeed, of all computers in general, although the games might only be a small proportion of the software on the largest commercial systems. In the case of the PCs, however, all of these elements are immediately obvious. When users buy a PC, they will always be provided with the operating system, which most usually comes with a handful of the simplest of applications and games included. In most cases, they will then also buy the more sophisticated applications, and typically some games. For many users – most obviously children – the games are in fact the most important aspect of the system.

All of this software, however, will need to change over time. New versions of applications, more sophisticated and powerful games, and extensions to the operating system are produced on a regular basis. A user that chose so to do could easily find themselves upgrading one or more aspects of their complete software set every week of the year. Furthermore, these upgrades and the original applications are typically very expensive – the most sophisticated computer games are between £30 and £90, and operating system or application upgrades are also around this mark.

This gives us the motivation for the illegal trade of these computer components: they are essential, expensive and tradable. As with the physical computer components discussed in the previous chapter, computer users expect to buy and to be sold these elements. Unlike the case with the physical, stolen goods, however, stolen software does not directly harm those from whom the software has been stolen: they still *have* the software; its utility for them has been in no way damaged.

Theft – with the implication of 'permanently depriving' the rightful owners of the property – is therefore different in the case of goods which can be copied. Those who steal and resell software can do so simply by copying the digital form of the goods from a victim's PC or computer, and then selling this copy to an unconcerned third party. There need not even be a 'victim' from whom the software is stolen – instead, the thief might in fact buy the original software legitimately, and then resell it.

The perfect crime? No victim, no loss? Well, not quite. This is, of course, 'bootlegging' or piracy – a crime against the owner of the *copyright* rather than the owner of the specific instance of the digital goods – and in the case of software, is estimated to cost UK companies around £540 million per year, and $15.2 billion worldwide in 1994 [*Economist* 1996]. Music, video, fashion items, pictures and many other goods are bootlegged. Illegal copies of the music, design or image are made, duplicated cheaply and then sold at venues ranging from fast turnover, back street shops to car boot sales.

Fake or illegally duplicated designer goods are a feature of very many street markets throughout the world – and this now of course includes software. It harms the owner of the copyright, insofar as legitimate versions of their inventions are not then bought – thereby clearly reducing their income from the licensed use of their intellectual property. It also indirectly damages them – their reputation, specifically – through the dissemination of poor quality copies.

Quality of reproduction

In the case of goods such as music, bootlegged versions are particularly obvious: they are all of a low quality as the process of copying the goods always introduces errors. It is possible, for example, to borrow a music CD from a public library, or even to buy it. This can then be recorded onto an audio tape cassette, typically for one's own use – say, in the car.

This first generation copy is not perfect: the copying process inevitably introduces unwanted, extraneous noise from the playback system, the recording system, and from the tape itself. With good equipment, the copy is sufficiently close for most purposes. However, second or subsequent generation copies taken from that first copy multiply the 'noise' in relation to the correct 'signal': the recording gradually but inexorably deteriorates with each re-recording, until in time the music (or video, or whatever) is of too poor a quality for further recording to produce anything more than random, 'white' noise.

In the arguably 'fair use' case of recording for one's own use, this is seldom a problem – although in the UK even this is not strictly legitimate. Illegal bootlegging, however, involves producing very many copies, and copies of copies, for sale. The end quality of this product is often so poor that it is immediately recognisable for the illegal version that it is; the bootlegger can then only sell the low quality goods to those who are sufficiently gullible or uncaring not to mind. In addition to the low quality of the *content*, the packaging of the video, cassette or whatever must also be duplicated, again with the introduction of quality-related errors.

In these cases, however, the problem arises from the manner in which the copying is performed. Music, video or pictures are reproduced by analogue means that can never duplicate particular, continuous values with absolute precision – they will therefore inevitably introduce copying errors, which then multiply on subsequent reproductions.

By comparison, digital mechanisms can not simply reduce these errors, they can remove the errors entirely: digital technology can support *perfect fidelity* copies; each digital copy is itself as good as a 'master copy' – and can be used as such. This facility for perfect reproduction comes not from the sophistication of the recording or playback systems (although these must of course satisfy certain requirements); rather, it comes from the manner in which the data is stored and retrieved from the recording medium – CD or computer disk, memory or even tape.

In the case of analogue encodings, the recording stores a *continuous* change in some feature of the medium: physical indentations in the grooves, varying magnetic field, or alterations in brightness and shadow on a photographic film. Digital recordings, however, are of discrete, binary values – although they might well still be recorded as magnetic fields or similar. Because they are stored as numbers, however, a variety of computer algorithms can be applied, just as the case with the transmission of data considered in Chapter 1. In particular, it is possible to introduce additional values alongside the actual data values themselves. A 'checksum' can check and retrieve all or part of a sequence of numbers constantly, until it has been retrieved accurately.

Alternatively, more sophisticated check values detect the precise binary digit that was incorrect. Since there are only two possible values, the system can itself correct the error. Perfect reproduction can therefore be ensured. Even where larger numbers of errors might be seen (such as in transmitting data reliably from satellites, for example) still more sophisticated mechanisms can ensure that errors are not allowed to pass undetected. The precise details of these technologies are, however, well beyond the scope of this book.[64]

Of course, this depends upon the additional, error-checking values actually having been stored alongside the data values themselves. In the case of audio CDs, while error checking values are stored – to allow 'normal' playback to be very accurate – most domestic CD players filter out these values at an early stage of the reproduction, passing a continuous, analogue value on to the amplifier and thence to the speakers. For this reason, domestic quality CD players cannot be used by bootleggers to copy audio CDs faithfully: the error checking and correcting information is not made available to the CD recorder.

By contrast, in the case of computer software, this error detecting and correcting code is a feature of the computer storage medium itself. All data processed and stored by the computer is retrieved from disk with the most sophisticated of mechanisms in place. While audio CDs cannot therefore be easily 'mastered' faithfully by bootleggers, computer software *can*.

Reproducing computer software

Stealing software and selling unlicensed copies is a very simple process for the bootlegger. It is necessary only to obtain the first copy – perhaps even legally, just as with the audio CD case. This can then be installed on the bootlegger's system exactly as expected. However, the bootlegger then copies the software onto some other media – perhaps even CD-ROMs if they have invested in a CD production system – and then sells it. The software itself is a perfect copy; there is no way of telling that the software has been stolen.

However, while the software itself has been perfectly mastered, the packaging for the CD-ROM (or diskettes, as appropriate) must also be duplicated, as must the instruction manuals and so forth. Of course, if the buyer is aware but unconcerned that the copy is unauthorised, the quality of such packaging is essentially irrelevant. Generally, though, the packaging will need to look authentic. This leads, however, to the motivation for use of the Internet to support illicit distribution *without* the requirement for any packaging at all.

The Internet already contains vast quantities of software that can be downloaded. On the whole these are programs that the author or copyright owner has licensed for public use without the requirement for payment: so-called 'shareware' or 'freeware'. Early versions of many computer games, for example, are distributed in just this way.

There is also a variety of 'paid-for' software available, in which the purchaser must provide a credit card number or similar, in order to access the download site; this of course gives rise to the potential for further criminal activities, such as fraudulent trading (see later). Other than the question of download speed – and hence transmission times and associated expense – the Internet is a perfect mechanism for obtaining software, ranging from games to sophisticated applications and clever operating system utilities.

The bootlegger can therefore take advantage of the Internet to offer the illicit copies for sale, allowing buyers to download a file containing the complete, illegally duplicated software. Some bootleggers have gone further still, not even asking for payment: 'idealists', despising the supposed high profits of software developers, have made such illegal copies freely available for download. In one case, many millions of dollars' worth of illicit software was made available through a Web site; the owner of the site was subsequently prosecuted for theft.

Perhaps even more worrying, the same hackers' tricks that allow paedophiles and pornographers to hide illicit material on other's host systems also allow the bootleggers to steal disk space. Hidden files, masked by the use of non-obvious – or even non-printing – file names can be used to store literally millions of pounds worth of stolen software. Many university computer systems have been hijacked in this way, used to provide a temporary storage space while the bootlegger arranges distribution of the goods.

The worry, of course, is the extent of responsibility that lies with the computer owner in the event of such illicit, unauthorised and illegal use of their services; we will look at the legality and questions of responsibility in the following chapter.

Non-payment of duty

In addition to this illicit distribution of software – or indeed, of *any* digital goods – even the legitimate sale and distribution can potentially give rise to criminal activity, certainly within the UK context. This can result from the uncertain status of import or VAT duties payable on those software goods.

Software distributed in the traditional way, ie physical retail of CD-ROMs or diskettes in shops, has two elements that are important for taxation or duties: the packaging itself counts as goods, and the software either as services or as goods depending upon its nature. In the case of software distributed over the Internet, there is no physical packaging involved – this is one of its benefits – and so the software itself is the only important component.

In the case of 'pure' software, ie a package of programs and of utilities that perform computational work on behalf of the user – this counts as services. Where the software includes so-called 'audio-visual' elements, ie scanned pictures or encoded sounds, such as an on-line encyclopaedia might, then it counts as goods.[65]

Sophisticated multimedia applications or games might there-fore be seen as goods, but straightforward applications for word processing or similar might be seen as services. Where the soft-ware is downloaded from a UK site, this distinction is not immediately relevant: VAT is still payable in either case, and the Internet retailer can anyway easily be audited by HM Customs & Excise. Where the software is downloaded from overseas – particularly from outside the European Union, as will usually be the case (most software is downloaded from the US) – this distinc-tion becomes more important: services do not count for import duty, whereas goods do.

These questions can produce some interesting potential aspects. In the UK, for example, books are currently zero-rated for VAT. Downloaded over the Internet from a UK distributor, however, an on-line book would count as a service, and be taxed as such – but imported from the US it would not accrue any duties.

Word processing packages that include a selection of scanned pictures that can be included within documents might well be counted as having an audio-visual element, and therefore be eligible for import duty.[66] Without precise knowledge of the contents of the software or digital goods, the importer (the buyer, that is) would be unable to make their own assessment of the duties or taxes payable; it is not unreasonable to assume that such duties will therefore be overlooked – a *criminal* action.

While the VAT aspect of this importation is not a feature of digital trade in the US, the various state 'purchase taxes' *are* relevant. Although the underlying justification for them is not related to that for the UK's Value Added Taxes, the application of the various US purchase taxes is similar in many ways to the European case. And just like the situation in the UK, it is entirely possible to move digital goods between states – perhaps without even noticing; again, it is unlikely that the relevant taxes will be paid faithfully in every case.

From the perspective of the authorities, policing such activity is particularly difficult: digital goods are imported as packets of binary elements, indistinguishable from the countless millions of others that flow through the network at any moment in time.

Intellectual property theft

The final category of concern in the area of downloading software lies in the theft of the intellectual property represented by the digital goods. While the software can be duplicated easily and bootlegged, it is also possible for the programs themselves to be stolen – or rather, for the programming *ideas* and methods that they represent to be stolen by a competitor company. When software is bought, whether it is downloaded from the Internet or installed from a CD-ROM, the buyer not only has a license to use the software, they also have the software itself. Not only that, by definition the software is in a form in which it can be accessed and read – otherwise the buyer's computer wouldn't be able to execute it. Because of this, the buyer can begin not simply to use the software, but also to understand the way it operates.

Executable programs are specially structured binary files: a string of 1s and 0s that the computer can interpret as instructions to execute or as data to be acted upon. The original text of these programs, however, is written in a higher-level language – a symbolic language such as C, Pascal *et al*, or a more machine-specific language such as 'assembler'.

In C and Pascal, instructions and operations are represented in a manner that is close to ordinary English useage: 'if condition **then** action **else** action', '**while** condition **do** action', etc.

By contrast, assembler language instructions are expressions of the underlying computer operation that might be performed: '**load**', '**jump**', etc. There is a direct – so-called 'one-to-one' – correspondence between the assembler instruction and the machine instruction it represents.

Because of this correspondence, the binary, machine language instructions can be transformed back into the assembler language from which they were generated. In most cases, it is not possible to recapture the symbolic names that the assembler language program gave to particular labels or data items,[67] but it is always possible to generate a form of the original, perhaps with sequentially chosen label names. This is then sufficient for a suitably expert programmer to establish the specific algorithms used – and in some cases, even to establish the higher-level language instructions that might have formed the original.

If the software contained clever algorithms, such 'reverse engineering' allows competitors to identify and possibly even to duplicate the tricks used. This type of 'criminal' activity is a commonplace in all other fields: chemical companies buy and analyse their competitors 'wonder drugs'; new toys are quickly duplicated; and the fashion world generates design copies almost before the models have left the catwalk.

In the case of software, licences often explicitly outlaw such reverse engineering – and many producers put 'fingerprints' within the code. These (mentioned above) are unique 'mistakes' or programming features which – if found to have been duplicated by their competitor – allow the owner of the intellectual property represented by the special algorithm to argue that their work has been illegally copied. Useless but idiosyncratic sequences of jumps, specially encoded messages within the data items and many other subtle ruses have all been used to achieve this simple level of protection from illegal reverse engineering.

Such 'fingerprinting' is the most obvious, first step in preventing the illicit copying and intellectual piracy. More sophisticated mechanisms have also been produced, relying on encryption mechanisms to ensure that the copying is detectable and also impractical. For example, by encoding credit card details or other unique identifiers into encrypted software or digital goods, the data can be indelibly marked with the identity of the buyer. If it is then copied and distributed, the owner and publisher can at least discover the initial culprit.

Further encryption, however, can also ensure that the data is accessible only upon receipt of a unique, one-time key from the publisher – making pirated software impossible unless the key production mechanism can be duplicated.

Hackers have a long history of breaking such encryption mechanisms, but manufacturers can provide an escalating level of protection by gradually implementing ever more sophisticated systems. Illegal activities within the Internet can, however, stretch much further than the stealing of software or non-payment of import duties – in particular, it can be directed at those users who would like to use the Internet as though it were directly analogous to a 'real-world' high street.

FRAUD ON THE INTERNET

In the case of bootleg software, the capacity for downloading digital goods – specifically, applications and computer games – was of central importance; in the case of computer pornography, the essential anonymity of Internet communication and use was seen similarly to be of relevance. In the operation of fraudulent companies or individual 'con-artists', these two elements combine: remote, anonymous companies or individuals offering digital or 'real-world' goods and services for sale via Internet-enabled purchasing transactions. Fraudulent companies *can*, of course, operate in other ways in the information age,[68] but those practices which are most notable currently involve use of the Internet.

At its most basic, fraud is deceit with an intention to perpetrate a theft; that is, fraud involves 'fooling' somebody in such a way as to allow the fraudster to cheat the person of money or of other, valuable things such as information, time or goods. While this – in the Internet context – might therefore involve using certain of the hackers' tricks, it *is* different: the hacker was concerned with fooling the computer system's security; the fraudster is concerned with using the computer somehow to fool a real-life person – usually the computer user.

As we discussed earlier, there are very many frauds that involve using a computer, but only because the computer is the information age equivalent of the ledger book or accounts. Rewriting computer records, while it might be a *technical* challenge to perform, detect and prevent, is not a radically new type of criminal activity.

By contrast, while the Internet frauds are – as we shall see – essentially similar to the real-world frauds with which the authorities already have significant levels of experience, the use of the Internet technology *does* introduce sufficient novelty to make the frauds of wider interest and relevance in the context of this book.

Types of fraud

The most fundamental of frauds within the Internet take place between traders that would appear to be legitimate, and *bona fide* purchasers of the digital goods that are offered for sale. These goods (as we have alluded to above) fall into several categories.

Physical goods

The first category are the physical goods, that are distributed via a 'real-world' mechanism. This is the Internet equivalent of the mail order business – and of course suffers from the same types of frauds and illegal practices that can arise in any unregulated mail order procedure.

In this case, the goods that are offered might be stolen (less 'fraudulent' trade, and more 'fencing' of property); the goods might be described in a false or misleading manner (again, not so much 'fraudulent' trading as a matter for the advertising standards regulators); or the trader could even be representing his- or herself as a particular organisation (say, Harrods) but being in fact entirely unconnected (a type of fraud referred to as 'passing off').[69]

More strictly fraudulent, the trader might take orders and payment for the physical goods. They might well then not deliver the goods – either because the goods don't exist, or because of some import restriction of which the buyer was unaware; or they might deliver the wrong goods, and subsequently be unavailable to provide recompense.

Digital goods

The second type of trade involves the sale of digital goods, such as the software case examined above. In this event, the buyer expects to provide payment – and then to be able to download the digital goods directly. Leaving on one side the previously discussed case of stolen, pirated or bootlegged digital goods, the fraudulent trader could easily again take payment but then not allow the downloading of the goods. Either the trader's host computer could develop a persistent 'fault', or the goods can be apparently scrambled in the download process, or the transmission could simply not be undertaken at all.

In many ways, this is very close to the situation with purely physical goods but with the distribution mechanism supported via network connections.

Published goods or services

The third type of trade is for those goods or services that are published over the Internet. In the case of newspapers, magazines and even poetry and novels on-line, there is currently no expectation of payment – there is therefore little or no scope for fraud. The most readily apparent case in which payment for on-line publishing is required is that of computer pornography.

In this case, there are two types of fraud: firstly, the pictures for which the 'punter' has paid to access may not live up to his expectations or the advertised quality; given the nature of the pornographic material readily available, this is less than likely. In the second type, the publisher might choose to abuse the payment mechanism. This abuse, however, is the common foundation in all of the cases – and is a much greater risk (both potentially and in practice) than the simple non-delivery of goods or the sale of stolen property.

Credit card abuse

As with the 'real world', Internet payment can be made through one of several mechanisms: by the exchange of cash; by a debit token against an account – such as a cheque or notice to deduct an amount from a buyer's pre-established credit balance with a third party such as a bank; or by the provision of a credit card or credit account number. Of course, all of these can be effected 'off-line', but the more interesting cases arise where the transaction is wholly within the Internet.

In the case of Internet payment, this is most usually achieved by the exchange of a credit card number. There are now specific Internet banks, and there are digital cash mechanisms – such as the recent MONDEX experiment – that can allow cash tokens to be transmitted over the Internet. These are not as widely used for payment purposes as are the credit cards, simply because credit cards provide a degree of consumer purchasing protection[70] – and are in any case of more relevance in the related context of money laundering (discussed below).

Credit cards, therefore, present the most common mechanism: buyers choose the required goods and complete an order form or similar to actually select it. The credit card number, expiry date and cardholder's name are then provided along with this order form. A closely related mechanism centres on the provision of access to 'adult' Web sites, in which the credit card is used to buy an 'adult verification token'. In both cases, the credit card is of course open to a number of obvious abuses.

In the case of credit card fraud, the misleading element involves fooling the cardholder into providing the card's details. This is not, of course, limited to the Internet case: in everyday use, the credit card can be abused by anybody and everybody to whom it is given. Credit cards are passed to waiters, shopkeepers, receptionists – almost all of whom can take the card away from the cardholder's immediate sight and copy the number, place illicit telephone orders, or even run off double slips. The Association for Payment and Clearing Services, for example, in its Annual Review for 1995, said that such abuse amounted to over £80 million in 1995 in the UK alone.

The credit card companies provide advice to cardholders to guard against such activities – and ask them to check their statements carefully so as to detect any such illicit (or rather, illegal) use of the card. Provided that the cardholder has taken what one might think of as appropriately careful steps to guard against such abuse, they are protected from bearing the full loss – although of course, *all* cardholders carry the cost of such frauds, in terms of fees, interest charges and the associated expenses.

Within the Internet, however, the anonymity and remoteness of the traders means that all credit card transactions take place outside of the cardholder's view. The card details are entered on a form which then passes through the Internet to the trader. The anonymity of the Internet also means that the trader might not be all that they purport to be: the Internet presence of the most insignificant, backstreet trader can be every bit as sophisticated as that of the most reputable 'real-world' organisation. Internet shoppers have little or no means of determining with whom they are dealing. Fraudulent traders can therefore easily pass themselves off as legitimate and worthy of such trade, or even as being a specific shop (as discussed above).

The most obvious abuse is by these fraudulent traders. Having received the credit card numbers, they can bill the card company without then distributing the bought goods – or they can take very many orders, process them through the company, and then simply disappear; or they can process the orders correctly, but record the credit card details for later abuse – perhaps even selling those numbers to organised credit card fraud syndicates.

Card abuse need not, obviously, be restricted to the trader: in most cases they will be entirely legitimate. The Internet communication is not, however, particularly secure: it is possible to intercept transmissions at several places within the system, and to retrieve the credit card numbers. Most obviously, the ISP to whom the purchaser is connected has unconstrained access to the user's communications. All e-mail and retrieved Web pages need to be processed through the ISP's host computer. Each page that is retrieved or transmitted is 'cached'[71] within this system. The ISP (or rather, the ISP's administrative staff) can therefore easily access, and perhaps even change, the contents of these pages. This of course means that any credit card details can be seen.

In passing we might remark that, while the vast majority of ISP organisations are entirely legitimate, there is no regulation of their activities in terms of the types of staff that they recruit and employ. Anybody can work for an ISP – or even establish themselves as an ISP, offering commercial services of the most sensitive nature – an attractive proposition for fraudsters, blackmailers or worse. It is only necessary to lease appropriate telecommunications bandwidth and to buy the relevant host computers and software; they can then sell their services, while monitoring and acting upon any information that they discover [Lockett 1996].

This is not to say that such activities *have* occurred – but rather, that there is no mechanism in place to ensure that they *don't*.

The trader, the ISP, or the trader's ISP[72] are all, therefore, in a position to collect and use the credit card details illegally. Throughout the Internet, it is also possible for others to intercept some or all of the packets that form the transmissions and similarly to record and use the credit card details.

Because of these difficulties, credit card companies now provide specific advice *not* to disseminate card details over the Internet. To avoid these problems and be able to use the cards, it is necessary to apply encryption technology, thereby masking the credit card numbers and preventing casual reading and use (see pages 85–6). The credit card companies have produced just such a mechanism (SET – Secure Electronic Transaction).

Once SET is in place, the credit card can be used over the Internet with the companies' blessings – important in the event that the details are indeed stolen and used illegally. Without that approval, the card provider or bank can disclaim all responsibility for the theft, placing the burden of payment back upon the cardholder.

Beyond this illicit capture, however, the Internet also provides for a number of other credit card abuses: advice to fraudsters on how to perform 'scams'; lists of valid, pilfered credit card numbers; even programs to generate new card numbers and encode ostensibly accurate details onto the magnetic strips of other cards – either credit cards that are doctored to refer to other accounts, or innocuous cards such as supermarket loyalty cards, re-engineered to act as credit cards.

Misleading with the intent to steal need not centre on money – whether through the theft of credit card details, or electronic cash or similar. Instead, the fraud could involve fooling the user into providing access to valuable resources such as computers, information and so forth. In the Internet or broader computer case, this is usually a case of applying hacking tricks, or even simply fooling people through the 'spoof' mechanisms described in the last chapter. Persuading security guards to allow one access to office equipment; collecting users' password details – all these can entail fraud to various degrees.

Other, much simpler frauds are also easily possible. Begging letters, requests from non-existent charities, chain letters – even threatening communications: all of these are as easily supported within the Internet as in the more mundane, 'real world' contexts. Just as with the computer pornography and hacking or virus cases, the Internet can be seen as a 'dangerous' as well as an 'exciting' place. It is no longer the playground of the academic or of the 'anorak': it is as likely to contain crooks, fraudsters and con-artists as any other media or aspect of our lives; more worryingly, it can also support the most dangerous, organised criminal activity.

ELECTRONIC MONEY LAUNDERING

Computer chips might be stolen by organised gangs of low-tech criminals; and child pornography might be distributed among an organised ring of paedophiles – but this is not 'organised crime' in the usual meaning of the term.[73]

Organised crime – in the sense of broad, long-standing criminal syndicates or gangster families such as the Mafia, Tongs or the Yakuza – involves the coordinated execution of very many, closely integrated activities; indeed, in most cases, only a few of these activities need to be overtly illegal.

Drug dealing, for example, is perhaps the best known – or at least, most widely recognised – example of organised crime. Production, distribution and sale of the drugs themselves, while it might be a complex activity involving farming, pharmaceutical and smuggling expertise, is not the complete picture: once the drugs have been sold, it is necessary to process the money so as to allow its use by the criminals involved.

If the drugs were to be sold by street corner dealers, who promptly delivered the money directly to those 'bosses' controlling the distribution, it would be simplicity itself to detect, implicate and successfully prosecute those bosses. Very quickly, the drug problem in the US, UK and throughout the world would be eradicated.

Unfortunately, the dealers do not deliver the money directly to those bosses; instead, the money is passed through a complex series of intermediaries, and through an equally complex series of accounts and investment manipulations. Illegal funds enter a web or network of closely connected companies and accounts, through which they move in a series of very rapid transfers. While the money obtained by the street corner dealer is unequivocally illegal – 'dirty' – it is steadily legitimised through the complex transactions until the money that is finally delivered to the bosses is apparently 'clean'.

The dirty money has been laundered by its movement through a sufficiently intricate chain of transactions so as to inhibit tracing, and by steady intermixing with legitimate funds, or with funds such as interest payments that at first sight would appear to be legitimate. The total size of the illegitimate, money laundering economy is unknown: by definition the transactions are not declared; but many estimates suggest that the transactions approximate to some £500 billion per year world-wide [Warren 1996] – the economy of a small country![74]

This laundering of 'dirty' money is a feature not only of the drug dealing business: money stolen in a bank robbery might have had the serial numbers recorded or be traceable through other mechanisms; it is therefore necessary to launder these notes through a laborious series of intermediate accounts and transactions (hence, of course, bank robbers seldom see the full, face value of the notes they have stolen but only the equivalent of the 'fence value' mentioned in the previous chapter).

Similarly, counterfeit notes must be distributed carefully through a number of accounts, rather than 'dropped' in one or two easily detected transactions. And conversely, money provided for the purchase of terrorists' weapons must pass through a *reverse*-laundering process, to allow ostensibly legitimate (and supposedly morally defensible) charity donations or similar to be made available in the form of Armalites and high explosives.

Tracing of such funds is the responsibility of a similarly wide range of authorities. The laundering process might hide money that should be taxed, or that should be returned to its owner, or funds that are the proceeds of immoral or illegal activities. The police, tax and customs authorities, UK Serious Fraud Office (SFO) and many others need expertise in following, understanding and – most importantly – *explaining* in court that these transactions represent illegal laundering.

In each of these cases there are a number of common features. Most particularly, the laundering process relies on confusing the detective (or rather, the 'forensic accountant') with a complex network of companies, accounts, transactions, investments and currency exchanges. A chain of transactions that are performed rapidly, and most often involve moving the money between countries and outside of the judicial control of a particular authority, making it not only difficult to track, but also difficult to control even when it *can* be tracked.

It is important to recognise, however, that all such transaction chains can, in principle at least, be audited and tracked: where the laundering involves the movement of funds through ostensibly legitimate bank accounts (as it must do if the money is to become 'clean'), then an audit trail is always produced – an audit trail that is effectively indelible, involving a series of records within very many systems. In practice, of course, this might be so complex as to be effectively impossible to understand.

If indeed the network of transactions *has* been understood – by the investigating accountants, tax inspectors and so on, it is important further to recognise that their task is far from complete. Simply understanding that a series of account movements represent the rapid transferral of illegal funds is not sufficient – it is then necessary to explain those transactions in such a way as to allow a prosecution to be effected. This means that the very, very complex web must be described to and appreciated by non-expert juries, a problem that dogs the SFO, Crown Prosecution Service, Inland Revenue and others in persuading the Director of Public Prosecutions to allow the prosecution attempt to be made.

Why is this laundering process important in the context of information age crime? As with many other aspects, in most cases the computer is involved as a surrogate for an established paper-based record system; in place of account books and transaction certificates, computerised file records and database entries are used. The criminal process of laundering money would seem on first inspection to be an issue of illegal *accountancy* practices rather than special application of *computer* expertise.

There is, as with the other examples in this and the previous chapter, an element of truth to this. However, the involvement of computers and of computer networks *does* bring certain unique and interesting features to the process.

Firstly, the criminal can use computers to record, establish and even to control the complex web of transactions. The more convoluted this network becomes, the more difficult it is to identify, understand and explain – but conversely, the more difficult it becomes for the criminal to understand and control. By using computers, the complexity of account transactions can become arbitrarily detailed – although it might require powerful computers to execute the control programs, these programs can 'understand' complexity well beyond the ability of mere mortals.

Through sophisticated software to establish and to operate the laundering chain of accounts and transactions, the criminal can therefore ensure that the sequence is beyond the capacity of most forensic accountants to audit (although, as we shall see, the use of computer mechanisms is equally available to them).

In the movement and control of funds through legitimate – and hence audited – account transactions this is perhaps the limit of computer involvement that is possible. In the information age, however, digital technology is involved far more intimately than this. When the banks store or transfer the fund details[75] through the normal exchange of money between bank accounts or in the complex networks of transactions involved in money laundering, they use digital records. These are held in bank computers, or transmitted in an encrypted format over private, international networks. These also contain and update the audit trails upon which the forensic accountant relies when tracing the movement of illegal funds.

It would be a mistake to assume that these computers and computer networks are immune from the attention of the criminal. Computer security can *always* be broken in some fashion. The organised criminal syndicate, for example, can obtain access to the banking systems either through hiring sufficiently expert hackers – or most obviously by kidnapping, torturing, bribing or simply forcing bank officials, system administrators or similar to provide them with that access.

In passing, we might remark on this aspect of computer security: both technology *and* personnel are important in the establishment and maintenance of such secure systems, and it is all too easy for technologists (on both sides of the criminal fence) to ignore the human element.

Accessing the banking systems directly would then allow the criminals to perform a series of modifications to the transactions – most obviously, details can be amended, perhaps even while the funds are being transmitted between banks. It would even be possible to generate funds artificially (electronic counterfeiting) with sufficient access to the systems.

In all cases, however, the carefully constructed audit trail will record and provide evidence for such manipulation. This audit trail is not a simple one-line record of a transaction, but rather a complicated and interlocking series of entries in several, physically distributed databases and even paper printouts. It is not *impossible* that the criminal could succeed in erasing or modifying all such audit records, but as Chapter 5 will explain, this would require access to the banking systems at a level far beyond that provided by forcing one – or even a dozen – of the bank's staff or computer systems to cooperate with the venture. In most cases, therefore, even with this type of computer crime, a record of the illegal activities will be retained.

As well as the use of computers and computer networks by established banks for recording and transmitting money, such networks are also now available more widely with the rapid growth of Internet trading and even Internet banking provision.[76] This aspect of the financial system – not simply within the US or UK, but now throughout the world – gives even more criminal potential.

As we have discussed above, the Internet now provides a variety of opportunities for purchasing goods or services in an electronic fashion. This requires the establishment of payment mechanisms, most obviously the secure exchange of credit card details. However, there are also a growing number of electronic *cash* mechanisms that allow the exchange of money rather than credit references.

In the Internet context, two types of digital cash mechanisms have been established. The first of these is a token system: an electronic record, suitably encrypted, represents some or all of 'real-world' funds held within a bank account. The user of the funds buys these tokens, the cash for which is therefore held at some central (and incidentally, well audited) site. When the electronic purchase is made, the token is passed to the trader over the Internet, who in turn passes it to the bank. Here, the digital token is validated for authenticity before the cash is released from the account to the trader.

This can be seen as a *three*-party transaction which is well audited, with the ability to record, analyse and assign authorship of each and every 'cash' transferral. This scheme has much lower levels of privacy and of confidentiality than the real-world equivalent of cash transactions.

The second type of electronic cash involves *two*-party transactions; this is exemplified by the MONDEX smartcard scheme established by Midland and NatWest banks. While the trial of this technology in Swindon throughout 1995 and 1996 has not been as popular as they would have wished, it nonetheless demonstrated that the system did indeed work.

In this mechanism, an 'electronic purse' (the smartcard) holds an encrypted record of the cash tokens which have been purchased at a bank – or indeed, over the Internet. These tokens can then be transferred directly between cards – again, perhaps over the Internet – without the intervention of any third party. Because of this 'card to card' transfer, this second scheme is far closer to real-world cash, and maintains much of the privacy associated with coins and notes.

The capability to transfer such funds over the Internet, however, also gives an opportunity for more invisible money laundering. If some or all of the illicit funds can be transferred into MONDEX-style electronic cash records, these can be moved with the anonymity of physical notes and coins, but in far greater volumes, and in an untraceable manner: there is, in particular, no audit trail involved, because the electronic records move directly, without the intervention of a record-keeping third party.

In the case of MONDEX, the individual smartcards have preset limits on the amount of cash they can record – each smartcard, therefore, can hold a data file which has certain constraints and is encoded in a manner private to the MONDEX mechanism. However, by chaining together a file containing very many such individual smartcard data files, much larger quantities of electronic cash might be recorded and transmitted over the Internet for storing in a locally held file, or encoding onto another smartcard so as to allow it to be used, or even delivered into a new bank account exactly as though it were physical cash. This money need only pass through an auditing point in the event that it is exchanged between currencies, but if the simple movement of funds is all that is required, such an exchange is unnecessary.

To inhibit such money laundering exercises, the MONDEX mechanism in particular (which is as safe as it is possible for the banks to make it) involves close cooperation between the smartcard and an associated bank account. This is to try and maintain a degree of control over the movement of large quantities of such money.

The sophisticated encoding and encryption mechanisms are also closely guarded, but a recurring feature of digital technology and security in particular is the apparent ease with which such ostensibly safe systems are accessed and modified by the determined or well informed hacker. It would be unrealistic to expect – although we can of course hope – that MONDEX or other digital cash mechanisms will remain safe from the attentions of the hackers and organised criminals.

As such electronic cash ventures proceed – and they are being developed throughout the world – one can expect a great deal of criminal and hacking attention to be paid to the encryption and encoding systems used. It is interesting to note that at least some of the digital cash experiments are being performed in the expectation that such encryption is more secure than the physical notes, which might be easily forged.

The reward for breaking these security measures, however, would be the ability to steal or to counterfeit electronic cash in the simplest, cleanest and safest possible manner. This is perhaps a much more attractive proposition than breaking security at the Pentagon's computers,[77] planting logic bombs and viruses in banking systems, and the host of other once seemingly impossible ventures in avoiding security mechanisms.

Perhaps more than any other feature of the information age, the introduction of electronic cash and the ease with which international telecommunication networks can be used to move such funds gives great potential for criminal exploitation. The criminals themselves need not have the high levels of technical knowledge required – organised crime can buy or extort such skills as easily as they find expert drivers, gunmen, surgeons and accountants: money talks, or families can be threatened. The same is true, of course, in the case of the use of such computer skills by terrorists, 'foreign powers' or fringe religions. Computers have become a central part of our daily lives – and the ability to manipulate those computers is now widespread.

SUMMARY – CRIME SUPPORTED BY COMPUTERS

Computers are tools, albeit sophisticated and intelligent ones. As tools, however, they can be used as easily for illegal as for legitimate purposes: they can be used by paedophiles, by vandals, terrorists, smugglers and drug dealers; they can be used to forge, steal or manipulate money – and they can be used in warfare, espionage and a host of the less savoury aspects of our modern lives. As they become ever more widespread, ever more people are presented with the opportunity to use these tools – and while the majority of uses might be entirely legitimate, there will always remain those which are immoral, amoral or even entirely indefensible.

An important theme that has run through this and the previous chapter, however, needs to be recognised explicitly: while computers might be the target or the tool for criminal activity, in all cases that activity is carried out not by technology, but by *people* manipulating or using that technology.

This is not the self-evident observation that it might at first seem to be. In many cases, 'the Internet', 'computer viruses' or just 'computers' are blamed for a variety of the unpalatable aspects of the late 20th century. But the Internet is *just* a computer network; computers are *just* harmless electronics – in all cases, it is necessary for the tool to be manipulated by a user, perhaps motivated by mischief, greed or a host of less obvious, or in some situations, unimaginable impulses.

In many cases, the detectives, the prosecutors, the security administrators – and even the hackers, paedophiles and criminals themselves lose track of this simple feature. Because the most apparent aspects of computer crimes and computer security are technological, there is an expectation that they can be addressed only through technology – but as the previous section discussed, organised crime can break computer security more readily by forcing those who already have legitimate access to furnish them passwords *et al*. It is not always necessary to hack.

This technological fixation is also readily apparent in the attitude of the hackers and computer misusers towards those who try to prevent or to detect their activities. It is interesting to note that once the hackers in particular are caught, they then seemed possessed of a seemingly unavoidable urge to educate the police or security managers – to try and show exactly how brilliant they, the hackers, have been; and to show that they are better in some ways than the police who hunt them.

There is an obvious and palpable feeling prevalent among the hacker community that the police and others are dullards – that the authorities are unable to prevent or even to *comprehend* the hackers', paedophiles' or others' use of the computer technology; that such use can be masked behind an impenetrable curtain of sophisticated encryption, encoding and related elements.

There is, of course, an element of truth to this – the criminals will always have a greater motivation to use the technology to its fullest. But equally, the technology is available as readily to the good as to the bad guys – and the good guys are fast learning how to use it first to prevent, and then to detect, capture and prosecute such illegal users.

This starts with clarifying the legal status of such unwelcome computer activities.

4

Digital crime and the law

Legislation – and the related regulation to ensure that those laws are complied with – is an important aspect in ensuring that digital crimes can be prevented. The Law is perhaps not always seen as an obvious element of such crime *prevention*, but rather as an element of the underlying justification for the very prevention and compliance activities that are themselves required.

In part, this perception is certainly true; but equally, the very existence of laws pertaining to amoral or damaging activities can also help in prevention by generating a framework within which the majority of (law abiding) citizens' activities can be performed. Without boundaries, it is difficult to ensure that one does not transgress against one's fellows: 'strong fences make good neighbours'.

In the context of information age crime, the existence of (or the ability to establish) these legal boundaries is particularly important. Computer technology and capability can proceed so rapidly that it is difficult to assess the legal implications of activities that those advances suddenly make possible.

In this context, therefore, there are three basic categories of law or of regulation that can be seen to be relevant.

1 An existing and well established set of laws to govern non-computerised activities translate directly, immediately and without the requirement for modification when applied to the

information age crime. The theft of computer components such as memory chips might be a good example of this case: the laws relating to theft apply to the act of 'permanently depriving' the rightful owner of their property.[78] This applies as readily to computer components as it does to other physical objects such as televisions, video recorders or jewellery; it does not, however, as we shall see, apply to information.

2 The existing laws *could* be applied unchanged to the information age context – but equally, they could also be strengthened by the introduction of specific clauses or by the production of an 'enabling act': an additional and related law that can be used in conjunction with the original. In the case of computerised child pornography, for instance, this is certainly governed in the UK by the existing 1978 Protection of Children Act, but this was extended by the 1994 Criminal Justice and Public Order Act in such a way as to cover very specific, information age elements – this will be discussed in more detail below.

As well as amendment or extension by additional enabling acts, these laws can also be extended by judge-made case law – in which the evolving interpretation of a particular act makes it clear that the information age case is encompassed automatically. Again, computer pornography that might be prosecuted in the UK using the 1959 Obscene Publications Act, together with the relevant case law established over several decades, is a good example. Similar and appropriate examples can be found in US statutes, either at the federal or the state level.

3 The final category is altogether more problematic. Here, rapidly changing technology results in a perceived requirement for an Act of Parliament or of Congress to establish a new and very specific law. In some cases this is understandable – the information age supports crimes (such as hacking) that are inadequately covered by non-computer specific laws; in other cases this rapid (and all too often highly emotive) response can lead to poorly thought out constructions. In the US, the recently challenged 1996 Communications Decency Act illustrates this particularly well.

In the main, while there are exceptions involving the most technical of crimes such as hacking, the existing laws in both the US, UK and elsewhere are sufficient to cover the obvious computer crimes. This is not to say that there are no bizarre, special circumstances or situations: as mentioned above, in the UK, for example, theft of information is not covered (information does not count as property) although it can be considered to have been misused or illegally published; this might be seen as an obvious area requiring attention, as it has in the US, where information theft *does* exist.

To address the legal and regulatory issues, we will not simply examine the major criminal areas illustrated in the previous chapters, describing the relevant laws and some of the key cases in each. In some of these criminal actions, the legal controls are particularly straightforward: theft of computer components is straightforward theft; money laundering is governed by existing, established taxation and banking regulation; fraud is fraud, libel is libel, and blackmail is blackmail – whether it is carried out through the Internet or by means of more traditional mechanisms.

Instead, we will look at the two specific areas in which additional legal controls *have* been seen as necessary, either in the enactment of wholly new laws, or in the extension of existing laws. These cover the case of hacking and other forms of digital vandalism on the one hand (new laws), and the dissemination of computer pornography on the other (extension of existing laws).

As far as possible, this chapter will provide a description of the legal situation in both the US and the UK[79] – in many instances these are particularly close; and even from a purely European perspective, the US laws are important, given that the majority of the systems, users and Internet content is American. A change in US legislation or in the way the laws are applied will therefore have impacts throughout the whole Cybernation.

Furthermore, a general approach to a common standard for Internet-related laws throughout the European Union – albeit not a complete harmonisation – forms part of a proposed European Commission directive[80] for consideration by member states at the

October 1996 inter-Governmental conference. This means that the laws pertaining to the use and abuse of the Internet in particular thoughout the European Union can also be expected to become similarly close.

THE LAWS RELATING TO HACKING

In the case of a multi-user computer system, there is an explicit list of people with permission to access the computer resources; moreover, for each of these 'valid' users, there are processing or storage facilities that they are allowed to access (or indeed, to modify) and facilities for which they have no access permissions.

In the case of single user, PC systems, there is a similar set of permitted users – although this set may well be an implicitly understood one: the PC's owner along with those additional individuals to whom the owner might grant that permission.

Hacking, at its most general, involves a user of a particular system accessing resources for which they have insufficient permissions, or an outside user accessing a complete system for which they have no permission at all. Conceptually at least, this might be considered as analogous with real-world trespass, or as breaking and entering – indeed, as we shall see, some US state laws make this analogy the basis of their specific anti-hacking legislation.

The hacker can access the system or information for any one or more of several reasons. Firstly, they might simply wish to gain the information held within the particular system or file, without then actually doing anything with or to that information. While the act of accessing the computer might be illegal (discussed below), the act against the information is not – under UK law.

This was established by a 1978 case between Oxford University and a student, in which a copy of an examination paper was made without the original having been damaged, removed or altered: all that the student removed was a copy (without the intention to publish). In the US, by contrast, such copying of information *is* illegal – a finding established by rulings in cases covering a wide field, from military information through legal to financial.

Alternatively, in the second case the hacker might access the information with the intention of publishing it – either for their own profit, or with the intention of publicising something that the owner would wish to keep secret. This might be an offence against the owner's copyright, or might involve the disclosure of information that is confidential or in some sense 'special' to the owner: details of a commercially secret recipe, for example, that is covered by the various trademark or patent property rights enacted throughout the world.

The nature of the information that might be published by a hacker is also relevant. Firstly, so-called 'personal information' – of a private nature relating to an individual – is protected in the UK by the 1984 Data Protection Act. This is discussed in more detail below. Secondly, the information might represent digital goods (such as software) that might be copied and sold – the bootlegging or piracy case. Finally, the information might be copyrighted material (such as music or software) for which the hacker does not have the relevant licences or permissions to support such distribution.

Copyright protection

In the UK, the relevant law covering the general situation of copyright protection of intellectual property is the 1988 Copyright, Designs and Patents Act; this covers a wide variety of intellectual property, from music, through literature, to software. It also covers – in the Internet or computer case – the owner of the computer (bulletin board, host, etc) and the user who performs the actual act of publishing, unlike earlier acts which did not cover such electronic publishing.

Where a hacker, therefore, illegally accesses a particular computer system and obtains a copy of protected information with the intention of publishing it, both the hacker *and* the owner of the computer they use for such publishing might be held liable. If, however, the operator of the bulletin board or host has no means of knowing that such an offence was being performed, they might claim 'innocent' dissemination.

In the US, which has essentially similar copyright laws, this protection would seem to have been afforded by an important recent case, known within the Internet community as the 'Scientology case' – more strictly, *Religious Technology Center v Netcom Online Communications Services* 1995, in which an ex-member of the Church of Scientology published copyrighted material through a newsgroup. In this, the Californian court found that Netcom could not be held liable for the illegal copying since the material was copied onto their host computers by an automatic procedure over which they were unable to exercise specific control.[81]

An important and interesting aspect with regard to copyright of software in particular is the question of *criminal* copyright breach. In the UK, a copyright offence can have two elements: the first such breach, provided it was not performed for financial gain, is a civil copyright offence – it is necessary for the owner of the copyright to pursue the offence through the civil courts. Subsequent breaches, however, are criminal offences, pursued by the police directly.

Because of this, in the UK, a hacker who makes software available for free downloading from a Web site (the *first* copy) can only be prosecuted for a civil offence. Those who download the software, however, are making subsequent copies, and so are liable under criminal copyright.

Most worryingly, however, so too is the owner of the host computer on which the software is stored: the computer might need to make several copies of the software throughout the process of caching or of backing up the main disks. Further, so too are the several ISPs whose computers are used to disseminate the software in the downloading process, and who are moreover doing so for *commercial* purposes.

In these situations, fortunately the ISP can almost certainly claim an innocent infringement if they were simply responsible for allowing a user to gain access via their computers. Where the material was stored on their computer, however, this might be more difficult to establish.

As with the case of obscene material (addressed below) the ISP is caught in a conflict: if they perform *any* checks on the data held by their users, the copyright owner could claim that the ISP was negligent in not uncovering the illicit software. By contrast, if the ISP turns a Nelsonian 'Blind Eye', they might instead be accused of negligence in performing *no* checks. A combination of close monitoring and effective user contract agreements covering such copyright infringement cases would seem to many ISPs to be the best approach – and is certainly the solution favoured by the more established ISP companies.

The US legal situation is essentially similar to the UK case, but commercial software piracy is handled in a slightly different way. In place of first and subsequent copyright breaches regarding software dissemination, the US law considers the value and number of copies distributed. Within a 180 day period, it is a felony to make or distribute 10 copies with a total value of $2500. Huge fines and lengthy imprisonment can be set against such violators, although there is still the open question of the ISP's responsibility and liability in this situation.

The third case in which the hacker might access information illegally is with the intention of damaging it in some way – either by deleting it, altering it, or by preventing its subsequent access by an authorised user (such as through encryption). This, together with the case of viruses and so-called 'denial of service' attacks (such as automatic diallers and e-mail bombing[82]) is covered within the UK's 1990 Computer Misuse Act. This act is of sufficient breadth of coverage and importance that we will consider it separately below.

In addition to the illegal access of information or of computer resources, the digital vandalism could encompass more definite, physical damage to the equipment: electro-magnetic pulse ('HIRF') guns that destroy electronic circuitry, even explosives or physical violence carried out against microwave towers, fibre-optic cables or similar. These – just as with the theft of computer components – are covered by 'normal' laws, although they might now also form part of any future battlefield, as Chapter 6 discusses. The interesting, computer-specific cases are seen as being within the Computer Misuse Act and the Data Protection Act.

The Computer Misuse Act

In the early 1980s in the UK, hacking was not illegal. Those who wished to attempt to access other computers or files within their own computer did so with a degree of impunity. Some universities stipulated that such access – particularly where damage was caused to information – was a disciplinary offence, but there was no legislative framework within which criminal prosecutions could be brought.

This gave rise to some interesting and bizarre attempts at prosecution: hackers would be charged, for example, with such esoteric crimes as 'stealing electricity'. Perhaps the most notable such early attempts at prosecution in the UK – and one which contributed greatly to the impetus to frame more specific laws – was the 1986 conviction of Gold and Schifreen at Southwark Crown Court.

These two were hackers who had managed to penetrate the BT Prestel system security, gaining access to the private electronic mail accounts of many Prestel users – including the Duke of Edinburgh's, for whom they left a number of harmless but annoying messages. They had had no intention of attempting to steal, damage or profit from this exercise – as we have discussed above, such early hacking was performed for fun rather than for profit. They were, however, charged under what might as first sight seem to be an almost comically inappropriate law – the 1981 Forgery and Counterfeiting Act. The thinking behind using such a law is, however, perfectly sensible: computer hacking involves 'fooling' (of computers or of users) and forgery of permissions in an analogous manner to that involved in defrauding individuals directly.[83]

The precise charge accused the two of making a 'false instrument' with a view to fooling the Prestel computer in such a way as to make it perform an action contrary to the computer's owner's (BT) wishes.[84] More usually, 'false instruments' refer to forged letters, cheques or similar that induce a bank to release funds, or to perform activities in the fraudster's interest rather than the bank's. The prosecution in this case sought to show that the fooling of the Prestel computer by means of what the judge

called 'electrical impulses which arrive at, affect and operate on
. . . a user segment' (ie part of the Prestel computer memory)
amounted to the use of a false instrument exactly analogous to
the use of a forged cheque or letter of authority.[85]

While the two were indeed convicted, their later appeal was
upheld on the grounds that the computer in this case was both
the 'false instrument' and the 'deceived' – there was no decep-
tion of a *person*, which is a usual requirement in the 1981 act.
In his ruling, the appeal judge made clear that the forgery act
was not intended to cover such computer misuse – that the
analogy with 'real-world' fraud and forgery was not sufficiently
close. A Royal Commission was therefore established to consider
the whole area, particularly given that the US had by that time
introduced their rough equivalent to the act that seemed to be
required in the UK: the 1986 Computer Fraud and Abuse Act
– although it was not until 1989 (and Morris's Internet Worm)
that this was truly used 'in anger'.

It is worth considering the US situation in some detail before
examining the UK act. In the US, the laws relevant to computer
abuse can be divided into two simple categories: *state* laws are
enacted to cover cases and situations thought to be relevant to
that particular state's concerns or experiences; and *federal* laws
are enacted on a more general basis, to cover those crimes which
have a greater than simply local impact or importance – most
usually, because they involve the movement of funds, illicit
material or even 'minors' across state boundaries.

The first of the relevant state computer laws was passed by
Florida in 1978; almost all of the states now have some laws,
covering issues such as computer trespass, tampering or the
manipulation of data – and interestingly, they also cover related
aspects such as simple possession of 'illicit computer information', including files of passwords. Within each US state, therefore,
it is likely that computer crimes (be they relatively harmless, and
therefore counted as 'misdemeanours' – or more damaging
and therefore 'felonies') are relatively well covered, but on a
'patchy' basis.

In addition to the existing state laws even prior to the introduction of the 1986 act, there were several federal statutes that could be applied. The most important (or at least, one with widest possible applicability) is the federal Wire Fraud Act. This law was established to encompass illegal acts that involve communication via telephone, telegraph, television etc over state boundaries. The nature of the Internet in particular means that computer communication – which falls within the act – almost always involves such interstate data traffic, giving federal authorities jurisdiction in even the most local of Internet frauds.

In 1986, however, and with a growing perception of the threat posed by digital hackers and on-line crimes, the US Congress passed the Computer Fraud and Abuse Act.[86] Among the concerns that Congress wished particularly to address in this statute was the potential for damage to government or military computing systems by means of such hacking and digital vandalism.

The act specifically outlawed activities falling into one or more of four simple categories, all of which required the perpetrator to know that such activities were illegal or require that the damage be deliberately and intentionally planned.

The first category involves knowingly accessing systems without authorisation, specifically to obtain restricted or classified government information; the second involves similar access, but targeted at financial information. The third is, however, perhaps the most swingeing category, making it an offence intentionally to access without authorisation *any* computer belonging exclusively to the US government, or adversely to affect the government use of a computer not directly owned by them. Finally, the fourth category involved knowingly trafficking in illicit computer information. In each of the cases, 'federal interest' systems were seen to be of particular interest.

As already mentioned, this act was most famously applied in the case of the Internet Worm. This case has given rise to adverse comment and criticism, most particularly by commentators writing within the Internet. This criticism has hinged on the question of the *intent* shown by Morris knowingly to damage the various systems that were affected by the Worm. Morris has always claimed to have had no such criminal intent.

However, at least some of the systems accessible to the Worm were of exclusive 'federal interest' – a fact that Morris, as the son of the Chief Scientist at the US National Computer Security Centre of the NSA, could not have failed to realise. The wording of the third category of offence described above simply requires 'the *intent* to *access*' such systems without authorisation. Since Morris wished his Worm program to populate *every* Internet-connected UNIX machine, including therefore those of exclusive federal interest, he hence had demonstrated the necessary intent – even if he had not planned actually to damage them.

On these grounds, he was prosecuted and fined, and his appeal refused.

By contrast with the US act, the UK act of 1990 was not framed with the special intent of protecting specifically 'government-interest' systems, but rather of providing more comprehensive protection through a deliberately worded act. Unlike the US situation, in the UK there is not the equivalent of state and federal laws – all laws apply equally throughout the country.[87] Before the 1990 act, however, there was nothing in the way of suitable laws – other than the fraud act discussed above – under which prosecutions could be brought against malicious or mischievous but damaging hacking attempts.

The 1990 Computer Misuse Act took some lessons from the US experience, such as the issue of intent and the question of seeking to access authorised systems beyond one's level of autho-risation. However, it defined just three special criminal offences in general terms, the second and third of which are arrestable ones.

■ Section 1 offences involve gaining unauthorised access to a computer or to those portions of a computer for which the person does not have authority. This is the most general of specifications, and can encompass hacking that ranges from quite deliberately targeted attempts at locating specific infor-mation files, to the most aimless of explorations.
■ Section 2 offences involve unauthorised computer access with the *intent* of then breaking the law further – by publicising

information retrieved, by acting upon that information (ie, in order to extort money or blackmail a victim) or by using the retrieved data to break security at other computer sites.

■ Section 3 offences encompass unauthorised access with the intention of modifying the computer's contents,[88] impairing its operation, or denying authorised users access to the computer programs or data.

Hacking with a view to publishing private, confidential or copyrighted information, generating and disseminating viruses, 'denial of service' attacks such as those involved with hostile applets, e-mail bombs or automatic diallers – all of these and many of the other, more imaginative attacks against computers are *all* therefore covered by the 1990 act.

For example, one can easily see how the law might be applied to a typical hacking attack: simply breaking security on one site and trawling for information such as passwords is a Section 1 offence; using those passwords then to break security at a subsequent, trusting site is a Section 2 offence; and then deleting files on either the first or second site (perhaps to disguise the attack) is a Section 3 offence. Those convicted can be fined, imprisoned or both.

To date, there have been only a relatively small number of prosecutions brought under either this or the US law[89] – the most widely publicised being the Internet Worm case in the US and the successful prosecution in 1995 of a confessed virus writer, Christopher Pile, in the UK. Pile admitted causing damage to several companies by means of the 'Pathogen' and 'Queeg' viruses, and was sentenced to 18 months imprisonment.

At least in part, the low number of prosecutions is due to a general reluctance on the part of businesses to admit that their system's security has been penetrated – either for malicious or other purposes; more than this, as we have already seen, it is often difficult, if not impossible, to locate the individual that should be prosecuted, and then to prove not only the hacking offence but also the *intent* aspect – a feature that is important under both laws.[90] In both of the headline cases above, for example, the accused had previously admitted the crime – moreover, where the hacking has been performed for the purposes of theft or fraud, many more prosecutions are brought under the Theft or the Fraud acts, which impose stiffer penalties.

A positive benefit of the computer-specific laws, however, is the clarity that they introduce for the legal position involved with such hacking attempts[91] – certainly within universities, which have in the past served as the normal breeding ground for new hackers. It takes the offence away from being a simple, disciplinary one and into the realms of criminal prosecution. In the case of the UK Data Protection Act – due shortly to be extended as discussed below – this clarity is even more apparent.

One important weakness in the laws, however, must also be recognised, relating to the *authorised* access to information by former employees. Once an employee has been dismissed, it should then not be possible for the person to access the computer systems. However, if the login for the individual is not disabled, it will be possible for them to satisfy the appropriate authorisation procedures – ie, password mechanism or similar.

In a recent UK case, a dismissed employee was able to access the company's computer from his home in this way and to take a copy of the company's customer database. In the UK, information cannot be stolen as such, and the individual did not exceed his authorisation in any way – the Computer Misuse Act has no power in this case.

The obvious response to this problem is procedural rather than legal: it is necessary for the company to have clear coverage of this situation within employees' terms and conditions – and to establish suitable 'dismissal' procedures so as to ensure that the passwords are removed.[92] More than this, to cover the situation in which *current* employees exceed their permitted use of the computer, it is also important to have clear statements covering the 'conditions of use' for the system – drawing attention to the employees' responsibilities with respect to corporate (and perhaps sensitive) data. This will not protect a company from the truly malicious hacker – but would provide some protection from the company's own staff, from whom the majority of security breaches are seen to come.

The Data Protection Act

To an extent, all forms of computer security hinge on the question of protecting the data stored within or communicated between systems. While this information can be of very many types, the UK (and as we shall see, broader European) law is concerned with a special category: *personal* data. This is information that relates to a living, identifiable individual – including aspects such as their address, income, medical history, sexual orientation, religion and so on.

A major concern in the information age is the ease with which comprehensive dossiers on individuals can be constructed by the collection and analysis of snippets of data available throughout the cyberspace of computers. The 1984 Data Protection Act (DPA) was developed to provide individuals with a high degree of protection and privacy from such exercises, particularly where the analysis is for improper or unauthorised purposes [Jay 1996, DPR 1996].

In most cases, a discussion of the principles of protection for private information hinges on the belief of a fundamental right to privacy – of personal information, particularly that which is sensitive in nature. In only a few situations would anyone argue against this most basic of protections. However, contrary to most expectations, such privacy is not a *fundamental* right – either in UK law or (interestingly) in the US, although it is recognised on a wider European front through Article 8 of the European Convention on Human Rights.

In the UK law, privacy protection arises most obviously in the context of moral rights introduced alongside the 1988 Copyright act discussed above. Specifically, this privacy refers to the unauthorised publication of photographs commissioned by an individual; it has also arisen (although not in law) within many headline cases arguing for a right of privacy from intrusive press and media attention; it is seen as an issue for *civil* liberties. In neither of these situations, however, is there relevance for the protection of private data, which has had to be provided in a special law.

The 1984 Data Protection Act followed agreement at the 1981 Council of Europe, at which *inter alia* the growing and central importance of information and information processing resources was identified. Most particularly, this treaty recognised that it was necessary to ensure that data processing advantages did not 'lead to a weakening of the position of persons on whom data are stored'. This did not formally provide a privacy requirement as such, but it formed the basis for the development of an appropriate law in the UK and elsewhere in Europe.

In the US, while privacy is of course central to many citizen's basic beliefs, such privacy is not afforded by the Constitution – or by the Bill of Rights,[93] within which most of the citizen's protection from intrusive government attention, for example, arises. Instead, privacy protection results from a combination of individual state laws and by a huge body of common law – covering such aspects as computer trespass and tampering.

In the information age context, there is also a relevant federal law – the 1968 Electronic Communications Privacy Act (which was extended in 1986 to include digital communications).[94] Unlike the UK DPA, this covers the illegal interception and publication of private information that might be collected by eavesdropping on telephone or computer traffic, rather than specific protection for stored, private information that might be processed and which refers to individual persons.

The 1984 Data Protection Act, which brought UK data protection into line with the rest of the European Union, would seem therefore to provide citizens with protection beyond that afforded in the US by the ECPA.

The DPA is enforced by a Data Protection registrar, whose responsibility is to ensure that UK organisations can be seen to conform to the broader European principles in their collection, analysis, storage and dissemination of personal data. Data users – that is, the organisations that hold or use the data – must register their collection, along with relevant information about it; failure to register is an offence which will be pursued by the registrar.

Once registered, the data user must then comply with eight data protection *principles*[95] – and failure to comply will equally then be pursued. In essence, the eight principles require that the organisations act in a responsible manner, and be aware of the sensitivity of the private information that they might hold. These therefore extend a comprehensive set of protections around personal data – although as we shall see, they are not wholly satisfactory protections in all cases.

In the context of global computer networks such as the Internet, the principles cover the illicit gathering of personal information, and the storage or dissemination of that information. The first principle holds that the data must be obtained fairly – in almost all cases, this requires explicit and informed consent[96] on the part of the data subject (the individual) to that collection process. There are many situations within the general use of the Internet, however, in which information can be gathered without this consent – for example, it is easily possible for ISPs to provide Web-site advertisers with particularly detailed information about those Internet users who visit a given site, and perhaps also about related sites visited by that specific individual. This is *personal data* about that user (his or her preferences), and as such should only be collected fairly.

While the collection of user statistics in general (ie, the total number of visits to a given Web page within a site) might well be seen as being appropriate and non-contentious, such precise and personally relevant data as 'who visited what site for how long?' – if obtained covertly – is unlikely to be seen as having been fairly collected. For this reason, those Web advertisers seeking to construct target-market profiles do so by means of registration forms, which *do* include an element of 'informed consent' and an option to refuse.

The data can also be collected in many other, 'real-world' situations: through analysis of purchasing habits in supermarkets; through analysis of credit card bills; through analysis of banking records, etc. In all of these cases, such collection must be fair, and the data can then be used only in a way with which the individual is content: in all cases, the individual has a right of access to that data, and can request that the data not be passed to some other third party – say, a direct marketing organisation. Only in the case of data collections relevant to criminal investigations or national security is such 'subject access' deniable on the part of the data user.

There is also a strong requirement for appropriate security measures to be enacted around private data. The eighth principle in particular states that the data must be stored in a secure manner. This places additional strong requirements on data users in the Internet context. Where their data collections are held on computers that are themselves available over the Internet, it is entirely possible that hacking attempts might be directed at those databases. Where such hacking has been successful, the data user would have to convince the registrar that adequate security had been in place or had been attempted – although the registrar will not, of course, automatically bring a prosecution in the event of such a security breach, unless it was shown that the security was known in advance to have been inadequate given the nature and sensitivity of any information that might be disclosed.

Although the 1984 act certainly provides a high level of protection – and is in line with European data protection, facilitating the secure exchange of data throughout the European Union – it is inadequate in certain regards. Firstly, the protection principles are enforceable only against the *data user* (or the computer bureau operating on behalf of the user) – but it is easy to conceive of situations in which data can be inadvertently released to an unauthorised recipient. The data user's staff could have been fooled, for example, into believing that a recipient was authorised when he was in fact an 'enquiry agent' (a private investigator, for example) seeking the data for non-authorised purposes.

Provided that the enquiry agent has not accessed the data illegally (by hacking) then the 1984 act has no powers against him, only against the data user. This 'loophole' (or rather, failing) was plugged in 1995 following the 1994 Criminal Justice and Public Order Act. Within this act, which effectively extended the Data Protection Act, the recipient of the protected data is guilty of an offence if he knew that the data was indeed protected; and he is guilty of a further offence if he subsequently offers that data for sale [Castley 1995].

This is in addition to the liability of the data user, which is in fact limited provided that adequate protective steps were taken: ie the enquiry agent 'fooled' the employee, through no fault of the organisation; disciplinary steps then taken by the organisation against the employee are not covered within the act, although such steps might well be seen as an appropriate response on the part of the organisation to such a serious breach in security.

The second problem, however, is that an *unregistered* data user is not bound at all by the eight principles; while such an unregistered user can certainly be prosecuted for failure to register, they cannot be held to the principles, such as the requirement for security or lawful collection.

Thirdly, the act relates to *automatic* processing – this does not therefore cover many of the most common manipulations of personal data, such as the simple display on a PC screen.

And fourthly, the jurisdiction of the data protection registrar is, quite correctly, limited to the UK – if, however, data is to be transferred to another country, the registrar has only limited powers to inhibit such data transfers (such as via the Internet) where it is believed that the transfer is to allow data to be processed in a way that avoids the protection afforded by the act.

In October 1995, these concerns were addressed within the EU Directive on Data Protection. This must be adopted by all member states by October 1998, and extends the data protection requirements of member states to cover the problematic areas in the UK's and other countries' individual laws.

One particularly important strengthening of the protection is in the context of what 'personal data' actually means within the law. In the 1984 act, the relevant data was defined as relating to an individual that could be identified – on the basis of that specific piece of information, when taken in conjunction with some other information *in the possession of the data user*.

In the EU directive, it is not necessary for the individual to be identifiable by the data user specifically, but rather simply to be 'identifiable' – ie, by anybody; in particular, by someone able to combine disjointed entries from several such, unprotected databases. This addresses the situation in which two or more separately held database entries contain private or sensitive information and are individually insufficient to identify an individual, but in conjunction would allow it – perhaps by the enquiry agent mentioned above.

In general, the Data Protection Act provides a breadth of protection for personal information equivalent to the protection afforded to financial information in the various banking and related laws. It has also been applied in such a way as to develop a wealth of case law, helping the wider and ever more effective application of the protection principles.

This is perhaps because there is an authoritative body – the registrar – responsible for ensuring that the regulations are indeed applied correctly and appropriately. In conjunction with laws specific to particular frauds or swindles, or more mundane activities such as software forgery and so forth, this and the Computer Misuse laws provide UK citizens with high levels of legal protection against the world of digital crimes.

In these cases, the laws were developed 'from scratch'. By contrast, in the case of obscene publications, existing laws in the UK and US were extended – quite modestly – to cover the digital case.

CONTROL OF COMPUTER PORNOGRAPHY

The laws relating to pornography – be it computerised or not – are reasonably straightforward, both in the UK and in the US – although there are certain special elements associated with the US situation, and certain difficulties in defining precisely the material that is to be covered by the controls.

The most fundamental element of the laws in both countries hinge on a distinction that few outside the immediate, legal fields would necessarily consider: *obscene* versus *indecent* material. In the US, this distinction has a close bearing on the Constitution – most particularly, its protection of free expression, as embodied in the First Amendment. This has very broad applicability for the expression of meaningful ideas: pictures, poetry, text and all forms of communication are protected from government controls. This protection does not, however, extend to material that is 'obscene', although it *does* provide protection for material that is merely 'indecent'.

Throughout all legal structures there is a difficulty in precisely defining the point at which indecent material (that might be thought of as offensive by some) passes into the realm of obscenity (that is thought of as offensive by many or even the majority). 'I know it when I see it' tends to be the attitude of many judges throughout the world.

In the UK, obscene material is that which 'has an effect such as to tend to deprave and corrupt' those who are able to obtain it – a rather loose definition that relies upon case law to establish the specific types of image, text and so forth covered.[97] In the US, a 1973 ruling provided a seemingly more workable test (the 'Miller' test), that defines an expression as being obscene if it satisfies all three parts:

- Does the expression appeal to prurient interests in the opinion of an average person applying contemporary standards of their community?
- Does the expression depict sexual conduct in an offensive way? and
- Does the expression lack scientific, literary or artistic merit?

This seemingly simple test is, however, very difficult to apply in general practice: it relies on considerations that are left to individual courts to determine: 'average person', 'contemporary standards', 'sexual conduct', 'prurient interest', 'merit'. All of these need also to be addressed within the relevant *state* laws, and applied with a view to the prevailing attitudes of those people able to observe the material in question.

This means that material might be unprotected by the Constitution in one state, but not so elsewhere depending on the community attitudes: California is generally perceived as being notoriously more permissive than many other states, for example; material that would offend against an average person in Boston might be seen as entirely acceptable in San Francisco.

Assuming that material does indeed satisfy each part of the Miller test, it then falls outside of Constitutional protection as afforded by the Bill of Rights. An individual state or even federal authorities are then free to prosecute the publishing act – either through their specific state laws or, in certain circumstances, a federal law such as that encompassing the interstate transportation of obscene material – which of course includes Internet or other computer traffic.

Both the US and the UK therefore struggle with the overall clarification of obscene versus indecent material, particularly with the ways in which indecency slides into obscenity – and the ways in which changing times bring changing attitudes. In both countries, however, there are then two specific classes of applicable laws – one covering the dissemination or display of obscene material; the second covering the general category of child pornography.

The Obscene Publications Act

In the 1959 Obscene Publications Act, the UK government sought to establish sensible controls on the general publishing – which included film as well as text – and distribution of material that (as mentioned above) would 'tend to deprave and to corrupt' those able to obtain or to view it. While this act was originally framed with the more 'traditional' media in mind, the 1994 Criminal Justice and Public Order Act extended the media coverage to include electronic. This extension is carefully worded so as to encompass the transmission in electronic form of material that, once resolved into 'human readable form', is obscene. Not only does this therefore encompass the case of digitised images, it also includes *encrypted* or encoded digital images – removing a possible line of defence based on aspects of technology.

There are broadly two forms of pornographic material that might be of concern in this context of computer pornography. Firstly, there is what is usually termed 'soft' porn: topless, nude or so-called 'glamour' photographs or videos, together with essentially harmless (ie, 'straight sex') pornographic text. In the main, this might be considered as being merely indecent – some might well be offended, but on the whole this type of 'top shelf' material would seem to be acceptable.

However, it is important to consider the potential audience for that material – the UK law in particular considers the material's effect on those people able to obtain it. Because the Internet is easily accessible both to children as well as adults, this might well result in a jury finding some of the pictures obscene and therefore illegal. This would certainly include ostensibly 'adult' images such as posed, simulated sex acts or even the ostentatious display of genital organs. By contrast, the more harmless topless pictures – such as those already well accepted within tabloid newspapers – would probably be considered inoffensive, even in the context of access by children; if they were not, the 'Page 3 Girl' would long ago have been banned.[98]

The same is essentially true in the US, with individual state laws addressing the issue of distribution of material that might be harmful to children – with various states applying varying age limits to define minors. In this case, even where the material might be seen as non-obscene – although indecent – it would *still* be an offence to allow that material to be accessed by children, although different states would apply differing standards of decency.

In addition to the 'soft' porn category, there is also an extensive category of 'hard' porn material available through BBSs or the Internet Web sites. This is altogether far more offensive and dangerous – given that, just as with the softer variety, it might easily be accessed by children or by those of unstable mental state.

Due to the ongoing attempts of the police and others in the US, UK and the rest of the world,[99] this material is becoming more difficult simply to 'stumble across' – but it is certainly still there. Pictures of bestiality, sado-masochism, perversions, mutilation and even scenes from what purport to be 'snuff' video collections – most assuredly material that would 'tend to deprave' (UK) and that easily satisfies the Miller tests (US).

Within both the US and the UK, the controls on obscene material (excluding child pornography) are addressed not from the perspective of the individual who happens to possess the photograph, say, but rather at those who publish, distribute or display the material. In the context of computer pornography, this therefore concerns the bulletin board operators (sometimes called system operators or 'sysops'), the computer owners or the Internet Service Providers who might be liable as publishers or as distributors depending on the degree of involvement they have in a particular case.

In most situations, the ISP (say) can perhaps exercise a defence – specifically, that they had not inspected the files involved and had no reason to suspect that the material was present on their system or was distributed by them unwittingly. This raises, however, some interesting problems – most obviously, the very nature of the Internet and its reputation for adult material arguably removes any prospect of a defence based upon having 'no reason to suspect' that obscene material might have been stored or transmitted by an ISP.

This means that the ISP is left with the option of turning a blind eye, or of attempting to implement some form of self-policing or scanning exercise. The difficulty, however, is exactly the same as the software piracy situation described above: a 'Nelsonian' blind eye might be thought of as insufficiently stringent, effectively approving or even of encouraging the spread of material onto the system; but conversely, a self-policing approach might well (or rather, will *inevitably*, given the volume of data to be sifted) overlook some material that proves to be obscene.

This concern is even more marked in the second – and arguably much more serious – case of child pornography.

The Protection of Children Act

The UK 1978 Protection of Children Act addresses *inter alia* the widest possible range of activities that offend against common standards of decency with respect to children. The act makes it an offence to take, or permit another to take, indecent photographs of children. More than this, it makes it an offence to 'distribute, publish, show or possess with the intention to distribute' such photographs.

In addition to these offences – that might be thought of as

applying to those *publishing* the material but not necessarily simply *having* the material for their own purpose – the 1988 Criminal Justice Act makes it illegal to be in possession of an indecent photograph of a child.

Storing, retrieving, distributing or making indecent photographs of children within the Internet or a bulletin board are all therefore covered – and those who might be prosecuted include the originator, the recipient and the Internet Service Provider (ISP) or bulletin board operator who facilitates that storage or dissemination.

There are several points of interest in the legal position of child pornography on the Internet or bulletin boards. The first is the standard applied. While the Obscene Publications Act outlaws material which is obscene, the Protection of Children Act outlaws photographs of children which are merely indecent – as we have already discussed, a much looser criterion, giving far greater scope for protection. Pictures that would be considered entirely acceptable if posed by adults (including many 'artistic' poses) are illegal in the case of children.

This illegality does not simply arise from the intrinsic offensiveness of the photographs themselves: in many cases, the photograph is also evidence of an illegal or indecent act performed against the children represented within the image. Quite apart from the pornographic element, pictures of sex acts involving children are also records of the sexual abuse of a child.

Certain software developments, however, in the field of computer graphics give rise to the possibility of so-called 'pseudo-photographs'. These are digitally *generated* images, produced either by the manipulation of existing images (a process called 'morphing'), or by the clever rendering of drawn images. Using such facilities, indecent, obscene, bizarre (or even, potential blackmail)[100] images can be produced.

These pseudo-photographs were recognised in law in the UK within the 1994 Criminal Justice and Public Order Act. To cover the concern of such 'artificial' (but nonetheless, still offensive) child pornography, the Protection of Children Act was extended to include both photographs and 'pseudo-photographic' images:

if the picture *appears* to be of a child in an indecent pose, then it is considered to *be* so.

As we shall see in a later chapter, the ability of computer generated images to appear indistinguishable from 'real' images is an important (and perhaps even dangerous) aspect of the information age.

The situation with regard to child pornography is essentially similar in the US. Individual states have varying individual laws, and there is also a federal Child Pornography Statute. An interesting aspect with regard to the child abuse situation described above for the UK law arises in the US with respect to the *medium* of the pornography. Images (photographs, videos) of children need only be indecent to contravene the statute; however, written text (since it need involve no explicit harm to a child) must pass the Miller test for obscenity – even textual descriptions of quite explicit child abuse are therefore protected by the Bill of Rights.

In addition, various findings of US courts have constructed similar legal positions to the UK case concerning pseudo-photographs and also the simple possession of child pornography for the person's own use. A 1982 judgement found that an image that appeared to be of a minor engaged in a sex act could be treated in law as though it *were* indeed an accurate image; and a 1990 case, that one does not have a right to possess child pornography of any form, even if that pornography is not intended for publication or dissemination.[101]

It is interesting to note a difference in attitude between the UK and the US in the attempts to police Internet published material. The UK's Home Office undertook detailed discussions with the ISPs and related organisations concerning offensive, illegal or obscene material within the Internet, seeking to establish a more rigorous 'self regulation' regime; the US, by contrast, sought the introduction of more extensive, legal protections – specifically, the Communications Decency Act. Both approaches are of course equally valid; but many commentators now view the UK's method as more likely to meet with success – particularly given the reception that greeted the US Act.

The Communications Decency Act

In 1996, President Bill Clinton signed into US law the Tele-communications Reform Act. This included a provision intro-duced by Senator James Exon of Nebraska in an attempt to impose controls over what was perceived to be a growing threat from pornographic and terrorist information within the Internet and bulletin board systems.

After the Ohio bombing, politicians of all parties and many commentators in the media began to draw attention to the volumes of unpalatable material that was held within Web sites and Usenet newsgroups. Directions for constructing home-made bombs, advice on conducting terror campaigns, and of course pornography all came in for criticism.

In an atmosphere of almost hysterical lobbying, the Exon Bill introduced restrictions on the transmission of 'patently indecent' material within the Internet, making the Internet Service Providers in particular responsible for policing the Web content directly themselves. The punishment for violation of the law would involve a maximum fine of $250,000 and two years imprison-ment.

On its signing into law by President Clinton, the protestations of the ISPs and civil liberties organisations began in earnest. These protests were based on two elements: the practicality of enforcing the restrictions via the ISPs; and the constitutionality of the restric-tions themselves.

ISPs argued – as with the copyright situation outlined above – that it was impractical to expect them to exercise either overt or covert controls on their users. The volume of data within the Internet and related bulletin board systems is such as to make the process of checking and verifying it for 'decency' all but impossible. Others argued that such controls would infringe their rights, would introduce an element of 'Big Brother' on the part of the ISPs, that what they – as adults – chose to view on the Internet was no one's concern but their own, and that protec-tion of children was a parent's responsibility.

Throughout the Internet, many thousands of Web pages were decorated with blue ribbons as a gesture of protest. To demonstrate that draconian laws were unnecessary as well as impractical, ISPs such as CompuServe also made parental control software available. This software provides a means whereby parents (and of course, employers) can prevent access to those Internet sites known to contain offensive material – although circumventing the restrictions is reasonably easy. The most serious attack on the new law, however, came from an appeal lodged by a coalition of ISPs together with the American Civil Liberties Union, the Electronic Frontier Foundation and other similar protest organisations.

In June 1996 – scant months after the signing of the Exon Bill – three federal judges upheld the coalition's appeal, declaring the bill unlawful.

It is important to note, however, that this appeal was not upheld on the basis of its impracticality – the first objection mentioned above – but rather on the grounds of the second objection: that the law was unconstitutional. Recall, the First Amendment to the Constitution extends protection to all expressions, including even the indecent, that are not deemed obscene; the amendment prevents the government from framing laws that impinge on these individual freedoms. Since the Exon Bill was deliberately worded around 'patently indecent' material, it therefore was an attempt to inhibit expressions protected by the Bill of Rights.

The judges even went further still, with what might well prove to be a prophetic ruling: 'As the most participatory form of mass speech yet developed, the Internet deserves the highest protection from government intrusion'. As the government and religious right wing protesters gather momentum for *their* appeal, it will be interesting to see the impact – and possibly broader applicability – that this ruling might prove to have in the information age.

REGULATION IN THE INFORMATION AGE

Quite apart from the legal controls that might be relevant to the information age, there are also a series of regulatory domains within which computers or the Internet are used. Within this chapter, we have already touched upon one aspect of regulation, in the context of the Data Protection Act; there are, however, regulatory controls over many other aspects of the information age.

There are two forms of regulation: that which is imposed by an officially sanctioned regulating body; and that which is imposed by an industry or sector upon itself – perhaps built upon the foundations of an official regulator.

Two particular areas of difficulty must be addressed, however, especially in the case of the Internet. Firstly, the global nature of the medium means that the regulatory domains of very many countries, and very many organisations within each country, are all affected. Controls that might be imposed in the UK can be undermined in the US, and vice versa; and the multimedia nature of the Internet makes it difficult to determine whether the regulations developed for the print, the broadcast or the tele-communications media are most appropriate – or even applicable at all.

Secondly, there is the question not of 'self regulation', but rather of *vigilantism* on the part of the Internet users against those who offend so-called 'Netiquette'. Although not regulation in the legal sense, this is nonetheless an important aspect of the regu-latory controls within the information age – and likely to become more important as the full 'Cybernation' of regular Internet citizens expands.

Looking first at the question of 'normal' regulation, there are several important areas that have emerged over recent years. The Internet can be used to support very many activities that are normally regulated in the 'real world': advertising, gambling, trading and the provision of telecommunication or financial services, for example, are all covered by detailed and well-estab-lished regulations within both the UK and the US. In each of these cases, while the Internet or information age brings many new elements, the existing regulations are essentially sufficient.

These mean that for example UK organisations or individuals, involved in the provision of services or goods within the UK, to UK citizens, via the Internet can expect to be regulated exactly as though they were within the 'real world' of UK high streets. Thus, an Internet gambling shop is regulated just like a normal bookmaker; advertising on the Internet is analogous to advertising in the regular media; Internet trading is simply a novel form of catalogue-style 'distance selling'; the UK 1984 Telecommunications Act applies to Internet Service Providers; and the 1986 Financial Services Act covers Web sites as adequately as it covers any other form of establishment.[102]

Despite the applicability of the regulations, however, it remains difficult to police these regulatory controls effectively – particularly given the global and apparently 'invisible' nature of the medium and its uses within official jurisdictions.

In the cases of self regulation, the establishment of effective industry codes of practice covering the Internet has been thought to be sufficient. This is the situation with the advertising industry, for example, where individual advertisements must comply with specific codes concerning such aspects as nudity or the use of offensive language. In the case of UK companies placing unacceptable advertisements in *any* medium, the ASA would seek alterations or even withdrawal of the material.

The global visibility, however, means that UK advertisements can be seen throughout the world, and the world's advertisements can be seen in the UK. In some of these countries, advertisements that might well be legal in the UK or the US could in fact be illegal: tobacco for instance. Should this offence be regulated by the UK's ASA (or the US equivalent for American advertisements)? In the case of distance selling, it is accepted that in most cases of unfair trading (and offensive advertising would likely count as such) then the laws of the country in which the *buyer* lives would normally apply.

This would mean that UK or US companies that offend against (say) Swedish trading or advertising laws in the case of tobacco can expect to be prosecuted under Swedish laws, in Swedish courts. Similar situations result in many of the other regulatable activities.

The question of 'official' regulation of advertising, however, leads inevitably to consideration of the Internet vigilante approach to regulation that would appear to be emerging in the information age context.

The earliest (and clumsiest) approach at advertising on the Internet involved posting inappropriate messages to Usenet news-groups – the regular readers of which took umbrage and replied by deluging the advertisers with vast quantities of e-mail 'flames', swamping the advertisers' computers and resulting in their service being withdrawn; appropriate revenge in many Internet users' opinion. This vigilante approach has been repeated in many other cases, where a (usually commercial) user of the Internet or Web has performed activities that others have found offensive.

However, a particularly interesting, new development in this vigilantism has emerged in the context of paedophile Web sites. Here, innocent Web sites have been advertised as containing child pornography; visitors to the sites have been recorded (their Internet address and user name) and then 'revenge' has been performed against them: denial of service and hacking attacks, together with e-mail campaigns alerting their employer via the Internet host system administrator.

As with most vigilantism, this might well be thought of as 'fair game' – but it must be recognised that the vigilantes are likely to be guilty of several crimes in performing such actions. In the UK, the Data Protection Act would require the visitor to be noti-fied and to give permission for his details to be recorded at the Web site; and the Computer Misuse Act, for example, outlaws such virus and denial of service attacks.[103]

Is the Cybernation evolving its own, internal policing role? Perhaps – but it must be said, this is unlikely in the extreme: for every vigilante that attacks such illegal and immoral uses of the Internet, there is another who defends that use, or who helps provide continued access to a 'banned' Internet site through the provision of local mirror-sites.

Vigilantism might, however, point the way for the effective, *official* policing of the medium – showing the ways in which, perhaps, the technology can be used to support both sides of the criminal gulf. For example, in the case of paedophile offences or the sale of stolen goods, the police could as easily establish such a Web site (a so-called 'Honeypot') and monitor visitors, using the information gathered as part of an investigation.

While some might see this as 'entrapment', there is a particular grey area around such police activities[104] – and in the case of such an emotive subject as child pornography such civil liberty concerns could well pale into insignificance.

SUMMARY – DIGITAL CRIME AND THE LAW

Computer crime within the Cybernation, most particularly where it involves the transnational aspects of the Internet, is difficult to control and to regulate. Despite this difficulty, however, it is apparent that a large body of law, within the UK, US and elsewhere, is applicable – even if the Cybernation *does* seem to fall outside of the national jurisdictions. While some of the more obvious crimes might take on interesting aspects in the information age context, activity which is essentially illegal in the 'real world' remains so in cyberspace; the 'citizens' of our Cybernation are equally citizens of the established states; they are covered by those laws exactly as any other citizen would be.

While we have seen that some aspects have indeed required the development of specifically focused laws – such as those covering computer hacking – in the majority of cases, the computer case of a given crime is covered by existing laws, or by modest extensions to allow new technological threats to be addressed. Although it may be difficult to bring offenders to book in many situations, the actual law which is being broken is usually now very obvious.

The existence of such laws reflects the fact that our modern, information age societies feel a pressing need to protect citizens, organisation and government institutions from the unwanted attentions of the hacker, the computer pornographer, and the software pirate. The establishment of such laws allows controls to be exercised – but they also, of course, impose a requirement on the authorities to ensure that the laws are not broken – and to ensure that where they are, the perpetrators can be successfully detected, captured and prosecuted.

Perhaps the most important, emerging lesson in the case of regulating such illegal activities, however, is the growing potential for using the digital tools *against* the computer criminal. While this has most obviously arisen in the case of Internet vigilantism, it is a realistic prospect on the part of the police or other authorities. The most obvious application of the technology, however, lies in its use to prevent such crimes occurring in the first place, and in the detection of those crimes that do occur. Equally, the technology can be applied in the process of prosecuting those individuals who are detected and caught.

5

Prosecution in the information age

In Chapters 2 and 3 a variety of computer crimes were discussed. In the main, these rely on subverting the protection that surrounds computers – physical, logical or human. While the implementation of computer security has progressed tremendously over the last few years, it is still possible, although no longer as easy, to circumvent or subvert such security. Because of this, the official response to digital crimes such as hacking needs to be based on more than an attempt to protect the systems – important though this is – but rather on attempts to collect information (*evidence*) and on capturing and prosecuting the offenders.

The laws described in Chapter 4 are of course useful only if the crimes are reported, the perpetrators identified, evidence collected and successful prosecutions established – without such prosecutions, even the dissuasion aspect of the laws is severely reduced.

This is particularly important in the case of digital crimes because, while the number of crimes is thought to be increasing, there is still a relatively low number of cases upon which police and court experience can be based. And in the question of hacking in particular, what prosecutions *have* been effected (mainly in the US) have had damaging consequences beyond the wished for message to the hacking 'community' – as we shall see.

Digital crimes – that take place within the cyberspace domain – might fall within the jurisdiction of several 'real-world' authorities, perhaps covering very many countries. Despite this, they cannot be ignored – they must be pursued and investigated. In the case of computerised criminals, this inevitably leads the investigative or policing authorities into the requirement for using such computers themselves – just like the police must use cars to pursue car-borne criminals.

This use of computers has several implications for the police, tax inspectors and others. Just as with the case of these computer crimes themselves, the information age technology has two potential applications for the judiciary: firstly, in detecting, preventing and prosecuting those crimes that are themselves digital in nature, such as the hacking case; and secondly, in combating non-computerised crimes. This second aspect is apparent in a wide variety of situations, from the use of technology to dissuade or capture speeding motorists (computerised traffic-speed monitors) to the use of AI (artificial intelligence), expert systems or huge databases in the fight against mundane, criminal activity.

In this chapter, therefore, we will consider the application of digital technology in combating these non-computerised crimes, before moving on to examine the particular detection, prevention and prosecution issues raised by specifically computer-oriented criminal activity.

POLICING WITH COMPUTERS

In the public perception, 'policing' involves the overt presence of uniformed officers walking the beat, dissuading actual or potential criminals by their very visibility. It involves marked police patrol vehicles; or armed officers at airports. For those unfortunate enough to suffer a crime – perhaps a robbery, or even physical assault – it involves seeming hours of laboriously dictated reports. And it involves – one hopes – ultimately capturing the perpetrator.

All of these, however, are dependent upon a crucial, determining factor: *information*.

The tools of cyberspace are vital in this activity. In the simplest such case, it entails the application of computers in the command and control aspect of police work – in assigning officers, patrol cars and equipment; in analysing and understanding patterns of behaviour; or even in monitoring football crowds, strikes and riots with CCTV cameras. But most importantly, it involves the manipulation of data so as to understand and act upon what is *known*.

Perhaps more than any other activity of the modern age, police work therefore relies on the ability to collect, filter, analyse and act upon information that might have come from such a wide variety of sources that its integration is a decidedly non-trivial task. The public perception of a 'detective' (a 'Sherlock Holmes', a 'Morse' or a 'Columbo') is of an individual able to abstract the *important* from the mass of data – a brilliant, imaginative, individual investigator.

Of course, while there is an element of truth to this, it is far from the whole truth. Most investigators are not 'brilliant', merely 'thorough': detection relies less on blinding insight, and much, much more on the careful, plodding approach to the truth – hampered by idiots who confess to every crime, by victims who are unable to recall important details, and by pressures of time. Detection is about collecting and collating information in such stupendous detail that the important evidence *must* be there – even if buried under a mountain of trivia; and most importantly, it is about sifting through this trivia looking for the 'needle in the haystack'.

For example, during the search for Peter Sutcliffe, the 'Yorkshire Ripper', the main police station in Leeds held dozens of detectives – but *millions* of individual, hand- or type-written information cards, stored in a maze of filing cabinets and desk-top, rotating card-holders. Investigators poured over an endless series of such cards and a mountain of interview and witness reports, trying to pull together 'threads' from the all too often conflicting stories. Sutcliffe himself, it emerged, had in fact been interviewed several times, but had been overlooked. Key evidence was found to have been hidden within the mountain of data – evidence that was eventually found to be relevant; or rather, was eventually *found*.

To ask a human being to collate and understand such a complicated collection of data – and from it abstract not just information, but *knowledge* (perhaps even wisdom) – is not simply misguided, it is nonsensical: human intelligence is not suited to such an exercise; but computer intelligence is. Following the 'Yorkshire Ripper' investigations, computerised investigation support systems became a high priority for the police force – embodied now within the major incident management system, 'Holmes' (the Home Office Large Major Enquiry System).

This is not only relevant to the police themselves – tax, customs and financial regulation inspectors must all wade through a mountain of raw data to discover the key elements that indicate a crime, and that can be used as evidence in a prosecution. In the financial world, millions of discrete trading operations must be monitored for the handful that indicate 'insider dealing', or that indicate fraudulent activities. Tax returns must be analysed, as must VAT, customs duty declarations and a host of other, mainly paper forms. Even within telephone companies, it is necessary to analyse millions of calls, in an attempt to locate and understand the fraudulent ones.

All of these aspects of detection and investigation point to a requirement for the application of computerised records and an ability to automate the searching, analysis and collation of information.

The components of the information age, the foundations of the Cybernation, can assist in this process in very many ways. Firstly, as we saw in Chapter 1, all of us now move through a parallel universe within which a mass of data is collected on a regular, ongoing basis. As we shop, buy petrol, and even drive along motorways, we are observed: CCTV monitors the roads, shops and garage forecourts; electronic fund transfers – that we use to buy our goods – pinpoint the location and time of a given transaction. To the investigator who looks, the collection of data is immense.

This data collection can not only allow detectives to follow an individual's movements, but also to begin to *understand* a suspect, or even a victim, in more detail. Just as the complex data collections of cyberspace can be used by direct marketing organisations to support precisely targeted commercial offers, it can also be used by the police. From the patterns of expenditure, and the choice of particular goods or services, an accurate profile of an individual's preferences and even their personality can be constructed.

As with the case of evidence analysis, however, this relies on the careful and intelligent application of computerised resources and software on the part of the investigators – on the use of criminal databases, expert systems and sophisticated artificial intelligence techniques: 'black magic' to many investigators, but a growing and important tool.

Criminal database resources

Perhaps the most obvious application of cyberspace technology in the pursuit of mundane criminals is in the collection of data. Criminal records, for example, are all now computerised. In the UK, the Police National Computer holds details on convicted offenders. These records can be searched and retrieved by one or more search keys – name, offence, address, etc. Similarly, fingerprints, photographs, even DNA records can be stored in simple databases and retrieved on demand. Criminal records are stored within a system called 'Phoenix'; proposals have been brought forward for a database of child sex offenders; and digitised fingerprints are to be stored within the 'NAFIS' system now under development.[105]

This differs not at all from the more 'commercial' application of databases to hold records of individuals – be they shoppers, customers, suppliers or whatever. In the case of 'criminal information', however, there is an associated requirement to collect and make available somewhat more 'nebulous' data. For example, data on criminal activities might include an explanation of a *type* of crime, or even of preferred victims – the *modus operandi*. This data cannot always be retrieved from the database by a search on a simple key term – instead, it is necessary to support more 'intelligent' searches, perhaps even so-called 'free-text' retrieval.

The UK's National Criminal Intelligence Service Systems, for example, contain a mass of reports and essentially unstructured data on known or suspected offenders. This database contains information about 'important' criminals – from organised crime gangs, to terrorists. In all cases, the information is used by individual forces throughout the country to augment their own intelligence and operational data, and must be retrieved in a very general manner.

The developments of database technology, supporting far larger, less precisely structured, and increasingly multimedia data items are therefore of growing importance to the police forces throughout the world. In the US, for example, the FBI and the Secret Service hold similarly complex databases of those who have threatened the President, or of kidnappers (a particular target of the FBI), or of the drug cartels, etc.

In the UK, the databases important for criminal investigations cover far more than the purely criminal or crime-specific information: there are large databases of tax returns, export records, vehicle licensing details; there are databases of telephone calls made from particular numbers; and there are databases of purchases made by particular credit cards. All of these are available for analysis in ongoing investigations – although 'trawling'[106] through them is not permitted. However, so-called 'Data Matching'[107] exercises *can* be performed – in a hunt for a given individual, for example, or for all those who travelled through a particular port of entry, etc.

All of these investigations, however, rely not simply on the establishment of large data collections – which are easily arranged – but rather on sophisticated software to analyse them.

Applying expert systems

The most obvious element of advanced software technology that can be applied in the analysis of complex information is that of Expert Systems – which have proven particularly suitable in many areas requiring the complex application of procedural rules coupled with 'intuition', such as in medical diagnosis, or even geological surveys looking for oil; they have even been used to 'psychoanalyse' patients.[108]

The use of the systems within law enforcement relies on a simple observation: police officers, tax and customs inspectors are all 'experts', applying a set of complex – and perhaps even subconscious – criteria to the information, evidence or tax returns under study. The 'Customs Nose' is only poorly understood even by the customs officers themselves, yet it clearly helps in uncovering fraud and abuse. Similarly, tax inspectors can very often discover the suspect or questionable tax return, and police officers develop a 'feeling' for crime and criminals.

Given the mass of criminal data that can now be produced, and that must analysed in even the simplest of investigations, an ability to automate this intuitive reasoning process is particularly important. Expert systems allow this.

These work by bringing together a complex set of obvious and non-obvious rules that must be applied in every case. One particular example might be that of screening tax returns.[109] This can be performed in a two-stage process: in the first, the complete set of tax returns is subdivided into three separate collections – a form of 'triage'.[110] Forms might, for example, contain obvious and apparent mistakes; these can be immediately separated and returned for modification or correction by the 'customer'. Alternatively, the forms might be obviously correct, containing no readily apparent mistakes or suspect items; these can therefore be passed for processing.

The third category is the one requiring further attention by the inspectors: forms that are, for whatever reason, suspect – even though they contain no obvious and apparent errors. With experience, inspectors become very proficient in this screening exercise, rapidly able to discriminate between the different sets. With the sets established, they are then able to dedicate intellectual and clerical resources to the second stage of the screening exercise, examining those forms that they believe – or suspect – to be worthy of further study.

The application of computers in this case similarly has two aspects. In the first, the computer program can be written with the specific rules embedded into it. These are the rules that the inspectors *must* apply: that particular fields have been completed, that data items add up to a given value, etc; rules that are easily specified and equally easily checked – 'rule book' rules, rather than 'rules of thumb'. In this situation, the only complex question is the manner in which the data itself is transferred from the (usually) handwritten, paper form into a medium suitable for such software analysis: data capture through scanning and pattern recognition, or by means of simple data-keying by entry clerks.

The second aspect, by contrast, is altogether more demanding. In this, the knowledge that is implicit in the individual tax inspector's assessment of 'risk' is uncovered and embodied in the system, through the careful construction of 'production rules'. These are sequences of embedded 'if-then-else' statements, that precisely control the logical flow of 'reasoning' that the expert system undertakes.

For example, a tax inspector might recognise that fast-food shops in a particular area of his or her district produce profits that usually exceed the national average, but only by a small percentage. Faced with a return from such an establishment, the inspector would apply this rule of thumb, based upon its address, for example, and if the profit was markedly less than the industry norm, he would recognise a potential error in the form. This is a simple case, easily encoded; far more complex cases are usually uncovered by a series of workshops with the 'experts', eliciting steadily more precise rules to encapsulate the specialist knowledge. This is often called 'Knowledge Engineering', and is itself an expert, 'black magic' art.

In some cases, of course, this process can be inhibited by the subjects themselves: few if any experts are comfortable with the notion that their carefully hoarded experience can be embodied within an automated system. Fear of redundancy, or simple discomfort with the procedure – even disbelief or suspicion of motives – can lead to tremendous resistance on the part of the knowledge engineering subjects, even where the experts are police, tax or other investigators dedicated to applying their expertise for the good of the broader community.

To circumvent these problems, while still benefiting from automation, two further aspects of sophisticated software can be used: artificial intelligence, and visualisation.

Applying artificial intelligence

Expert systems and knowledge engineering are both elements of the broader discipline of 'artificial intelligence'. However, in the case of expert systems, this involves primarily reflecting the skill and expertise of a specific set of individuals within an automated system. By contrast, in other areas of artificial intelligence, the system itself 'learns' and applies its own rules to the analysis and understanding of a problem area. Perhaps the best known such systems now rely on the use of 'connectionism' or 'neuron-net' technologies [Bingley 1995].[111]

The human brain is thought to represent knowledge – and to learn new items – through the gradual alteration in connections between individual brain cells, called 'neurons'. Each of the many millions of neurons in a brain (be it of an animal, insect or human being) is connected to a set of several hundred others. Each connection is one of two sorts: an 'Exciter' or an 'Inhibitor'; discrete electrical charges flow along these connections to the further neurons when a given neuron 'fires'.

A charge which enters a neuron along an exciter *adds* to the total accumulated charge within that neuron; those that come along inhibitors *subtract* from the charge. When in time the neuron is excited by sufficient charge – that exceeds a determined 'threshold' value specific to that neuron – the neuron then in turn fires, generating charge that flows along a chosen sub-set of the connections, and in turn affects those to which it is connected.

A complex, interconnected web or network of neurons, exciters and inhibitors therefore loops throughout every brain – the patterns of firing representing the brain's activity, ie thinking, remembering and reasoning. The more a given connection is used, the more likely it is to be used in subsequent activity when its neuron fires. Learning is therefore represented by reinforced firing patterns, as the network of thought becomes more deeply embedded in the biological matrix of the brain.

As an artificial intelligence technique, simple artificial neurons are then constructed to mimic this activity, either in hardware or, more usually, through software data structures as a large *network* of neurons. Input to the system – say, a pattern such as a face or perhaps even fingerprints – is then passed through the network, exciting and reinforcing certain combinations. Ultimately, this produces an output – it might perhaps be a person's identity given their fingerprints. This 'pattern recognition' by the network can then be evaluated: if the identification was accurate, the connections established are reinforced; if, however, the identification was wrong, the connections are reduced or even removed.

By this reinforcing of connections, the artificial neuron network can gradually 'learn' how to satisfy criteria that are never explicitly described. Just like real life, the network learns by example – and is 'punished' for failure.[112] 'Connectionism' is similar, but here the basic elements are not simple neurons that either fire or not, but rather more complicated procedures or whole programs that connect to others. The basis of the system is, however, essentially similar: successful connections are reinforced; unsuccessful connections are reduced or removed.

This, therefore, allows systems to learn in a flexible and responsive manner. It is not necessary for the developer to understand the principles upon which the system works – be it human or automated; instead, the developer simply needs a criterion for *success*. If the system meets the criterion, ie recognises the face, then it is rewarded.

Once the neuron or connectionist network has been 'trained', it can then be used in practice, with confidence that it will duplicate the trained reasoning behaviour thereafter, just like a growing, human brain.

Applying this to, say, the processing of tax returns or other investigative tasks is then straightforward: instead of eliciting expert knowledge, an adaptive, connectionist or neuron-net based system is produced, and given a series of tax returns to screen, or witness statements to assess, or faces to recognise, or even trading patterns and transactions to evaluate.

In parallel, these forms are also given to the human inspectors or investigators, and these are used to 'grade' the system's results.

Over time, the system would learn to become as accurate as the inspectors[113] without the requirement for a formal understanding of their reasoning.

While such systems have indeed been developed (although not yet for tax returns)[114] and have proven to be a great success in such aspects as face recognition or in evaluating fraudulent transactions, they are not ideal in every case. From partially degraded input – such as obscured or badly focused images – they can produce impressively accurate assessments. Unfortunately, they are unable to advise on the *way* in which the assessment was reached, but simply give a detailed account of the neurons or procedures that fired in a particular order.

This is an important point in the context of policing or prosecution, for example, where it is always necessary to convince a court of a particular expert judgement; we will return to this point below.

For this reason, however, other technologies, such as *visualisation*, remain important in police and investigative work.

Data visualisation

Data visualisation is a particularly fast-growing area of computer science [Tufte 1990]. This allows complex and large sets of related data items to be represented in a way that allows human reasoning to act upon them. In the case of the paper mountain associated with the 'Yorkshire Ripper' example given above, the data items were distributed over a wide set of media, and represented in a way that was essentially fixed: it was all but impossible to comprehend, let alone to reason with the information.

Visualisation techniques, by contrast, involve representing the data in a pictorial manner. At its simplest, this has been done for very many years, 'graphing' data sets to allow peaks and troughs to be observed. Modern techniques go beyond this, however, by allowing the *relationship between* discrete data sets to be observed: through complex webs, for example, in which particularly common connections are represented by thicker lines.

British Telecom have used this technique, for instance, to chart and understand the complex relationship of phone calls and message forwarding associated with telephone frauds. In this case, the thousands of phone numbers involved are represented as points around a circle, and the relationship between numbers by lines connecting those points. A simple technique, this allows the investigators to observe the most common and heavily used connections, and to concentrate their resources appropriately.

Police investigators have also used similar techniques to chart the relationship between suspects, or between items such as stolen property. It allows the investigators to 'picture' the complex relationships and then in turn to describe them in court. This is an important distinction as against the use of artificial intelligence techniques: instead of replacing, or even supplanting, the human investigators, the software is there to aid or to augment the human facilities. As we shall see below, this human aspect is vital in the case where prosecutions must be obtained.

Computer technology – the tools of the cyberspace domain – can therefore be used by the police or others to great effect, mainly to help understand or identify important aspects of criminal behaviour. These techniques are vital for 'mundane' crimes, but become positively *essential* in the case of the more complex, fast-moving and difficult digital crimes addressed in Chapters 2 and 3.

DETECTION OF DIGITAL CRIMES

As Chapters 2 and 3 discussed, many of the computer crimes are essentially evolutions from the earlier, mundane or 'real-world' versions. Some can be prevented by straightforward application of modern technology: the theft of computer chips is perhaps the most obvious example. Others rely on using computer technology to support the crime in a complex or new manner – such as the case with money laundering, Internet fraud or such aspects as the piracy of software, etc. And still others rely on the subversion of computer security principles.

Although many of these crimes therefore involve the *use* of computers, the detection of the crime is not necessarily always within the realm of digital technology. For example, it is more likely that computer-stored pornography – particularly if it is well concealed – will be uncovered by 'normal' policework (or even, within a company, standard management disciplines such as observing one's staff) rather than by analysis of the computer itself.

That having been said, in the UK, however, the recent investigations into Internet paedophilia (the so-called 'Starburst' inquiry) was prompted initially by observation of an Internet Usenet newsgroup discussion, in which paedophile material was explicitly offered. The people concerned appeared to be unaware that their discussions could be easily observed (and acted upon) by the police!

In other areas, it is also unlikely that the crimes will be uncovered entirely through the use of computer technologies – although these can of course help in analysing and understanding the activities involved. Complex money laundering schemes in particular are more likely to be detected as a result of alert tax inspectors than computer system administrators – or even accountants.

If an individual's lifestyle is obviously well in excess of his or her declared income, for example, the tax inspector will begin to investigate; and for organised gangs, it is unlikely that the police will not already have knowledge of their existence and activities through other means. This *might* involve the use of computers – for example, so-called 'badges of wealth' such as membership of elite clubs, possession of personal car number plates, even possession of a helicopter, can all be examined by inspectors accessing appropriate databases in the hunt for specific individuals. It is, however, far more likely that such investigations will be more direct in nature, involving interviews and analysis of accounts, or perhaps even testimony from informers.

In other areas, the computer crime only becomes apparent as a result of complaints: from a credit card holder whose card number has been stolen; from an individual whose personal data has been abused by a non-registered company; or by a copyright holder whose goods have been stolen and duplicated. In all of these cases, the issue is one of collecting evidence – discussed below – rather than of detecting the crime itself.

The investigative elements of computer technology only really become particularly important where the crime is based within the computer domain. For example, software piracy – where the stolen goods are offered for sale and downloaded via the Internet – can clearly be detected by observing the relevant Web pages or newsgroups. The criminal has to alert the potential market to the existence of the goods, and this can clearly also be observed by the investigators, just as with the pornography case mentioned above.

Of course, as we discussed in Chapter 3, it is entirely possible to hide illicit material so thoroughly within the Internet-connected systems that it is all but impossible to locate. This might seem to pose a problem for the authorities in obtaining evidence – but in fact, as we shall discuss, this has never actually proved to be the case. Hackers in particular are all too willing not only to confess, but also to boast and even implicate their associates; 'honour among thieves' is of course a particularly naive concept, so much so that even the children involved in computer misuse have chosen to overlook it!

While illicit material might well be hidden, however, the detection of hacking attempts, of virus attacks and similar misuse can certainly take place within the computer domain.

Detecting computer hackers

Perhaps the most worrying aspect of detecting computer misuse activities is the absence of a 'smoking gun'. A truly successful computer penetration would leave no traces – audit records would be removed or altered, access times on files modified, no damage performed against the data itself; no traces, and therefore no evidence of a crime. By their very nature, it is impossible to assess the numbers of such 'perfect crimes' that might have been performed – although within the computer security industry it is thought that there have been a large number of such events.[115]

Taking a cold-blooded perspective on this, should the police or other official investigators worry? Perhaps not: if no 'victim' reports a crime, that cannot be perceived, and for which there is no evidence, the sheer practicalities of police work mean that the 'crime' will have to be overlooked. With none to hear, does the falling tree make any sound? With no victim or evidence, has a crime occurred?

Clearly, it *has* – even if it hasn't in fact been noticed; the Computer Misuse Act says nothing about the crime being apparent, it merely outlaws the exceeding of one's authorised access to computer systems, whether for curiosity or in the pursuit of further offences. The situation is similar in the US with regard to computer abuse, although both Georgia and Utah states have imposed a 'duty to report violations' – making oversight illegal; in fact, these particular laws were intended to impose a responsibility on the captured hackers to report on their own or their friends' further offences, but they act equally against a victim. In practice, of course, the crimes which *are* noticed are the ones to which the police – or a company's internal security staff – will dedicate their resources.

In passing, we should perhaps separate 'noticing' a digital crime – such as hacking – from the related aspect of there being no perceptible evidence. While it *is* possible to hide access and audit tracks – most simply, by deactivating the audit logging process – in practice this is very, very difficult to achieve fully. Files retain a record of the last time at which they were accessed; directories retain an 'image' of files – even after the file has been deleted; and even the contents of the file itself will remain on the hard disk after it has apparently been deleted.[116] A computer that has been illegally accessed, or that has held illicit material, therefore contains a wealth of evidence, as we shall discuss below.

This, however, is distinct from noticing that the crime has in fact occurred. Unlike real-world theft, for example, digital theft does not always necessarily result in the 'victim' losing the item involved. And if the crime was the introduction of a virus or logic bomb, the victim might not notice the fact for some time – and as a result, much vital information (evidence) will be overwritten and lost in the intervening period. Where the crimes *are* indeed noticed by the victim, however, an even worse problem must be faced: in many cases the crimes are not then reported to the authorities.

Companies in particular rely on the trust that their customers place in them – including the trust placed in their computers. If it is admitted that these have proven to be weak, the company might lose business as customers realise that their personal details, perhaps even their bank accounts, are at risk through inadequate system security. However, a steadily growing public appreciation of the scale of such misuse and of the threats, together with a growing public awareness of the *true* situation, is gradually eroding this particular problem. It is *more* damaging to be found not to have acted against such penetration, than to have suffered the act in the first place. This of course makes it more likely that the police will become involved.

Beyond this issue of public perception, however, businesses' confidence in the police has also proved to be an issue. Specifically, the businesses (that is, the *victims*) have a very real and, it must be said, partially justified perception that the police themselves are unskilled in the area of computer crime.[117] In the UK, this might well be a fair perception: the numbers both of computer specialist officers and of successful prosecutions is very small. In the US, it is less fair: the FBI, Secret Service and military investigators have gained experience and capability very rapidly – and are willing both to work with and to educate local forces.

As the police on both sides of the Atlantic[118] become more expert, this perception of low expertise on the part of the authorities will also diminish – indeed, as computers become ever more ubiquitous, it is likely that computer misuse will be a growing feature of almost all criminal activity. It is therefore vital that the police gain this experience, and that the victims of such abuse therefore trust them (as well as their own security staff) in the handling of the investigation.

There are two elements to this detection of computer misuse: the first involves the establishment of computer security measures such as to allow the detection of criminal events within the computer system; the second is then ensuring that the record of such events can be admitted as evidence.

We have discussed computer security at length throughout the book. An important element will be recalled, that of maintaining a comprehensive audit log of so-called 'Security Events'. This is a major requirement in the case of those systems accredited within the 'official' procedures for government or military use – and an equally important element within the financial world. An audit log of events such as login, file access and so forth allows the activities of a malicious hacker to be recorded.

Of course, the hacker can, in principle at least, circumvent these measures. If he or she has gained 'root' privilege (which must be assumed to be the case) then they can delete audit log files and halt the auditing process; they can even alter the access values associated with the files they modify. There *are* simple means to protect systems from these problems: the audit log can be periodically transmitted to a neighbouring system – or better still, printed out continuously; sensitive files can be encrypted, so that they cannot be read; and to ensure that files are not changed, a size and contents summary file can be maintained (again, encrypted) to allow a periodic verification of their contents to be performed [Garfinkel 1996].

Because of these aspects, it is vital that, along with the audit, computer operators maintain an alarm or 'tripwire' associated with particular events such as access to the most sensitive of files or programs. Multiple levels of defence – so-called 'defence in depth' – is also an important element: it might not be possible to *stop* the hacker, but it is usually possible to slow them down long enough to track and record their activities – and even to alert operators who can disconnect the hacker.

At this point, however, the most problematic aspect of detecting computer misuse becomes apparent: what these audit systems, trip wires, alerts and so forth are monitoring is not a 'criminal' *per se*, but rather a *process* or series of processes acting on behalf of the criminal. Identifying the specific, human individual responsible for the activity is altogether more difficult.

Identifying the hacker

When a user accesses a computer system, they are assigned a 'user identifier' or *uid*. This uid is determined by consideration of the user's login name and password at the authorisation and authentication stage – it is assumed that only the valid user will be able to satisfy this check, whether by means of a simple password, or through more complicated, biometric assessment. By whatever means, however, following authentication that the user *is* who they claim to be, thereafter the system relies on the uid value in tracing the user's activity.

Audit logs therefore record the programs that the uid initiated, the files that were accessed, and the relevant security events that occurred, all associated with that uid. Along with the uid, a record of the type of connection to the system is also maintained. This is a 'port number', which might correspond to a particular terminal within the company's building, or it might be a dial-in telephone modem line, or it might be a network connection from the company's local area network, or from the wider world.

In most cases of accidental security breach (and these are by far the majority) this is entirely sufficient: a record of the uid and terminal from which an accidental but damaging act is initiated. In the case of hackers – or worse, of viruses – this is identification is not always so straightforward. Taking the case of the hacker, they might have purloined the login account, so that the uid refers not to *them*, but rather to their unfortunate victim. Furthermore, if they have dialled in, or come in over network connections, actually physically locating them might also be very difficult.

In the worst case, the hacker will be insulated by an onion-skin of nested connections, so that tracing the uid and port number to a remote system or telephone number is not sufficient: it becomes necessary to trace the connection back further still – through an increasingly complex maze of connections. It *is* possible – indeed, both [Stoll 1991] and [Shimomura 1996] describe the process in some detail – but it is very, very difficult, and potentially very costly in practice.

For this reason, most computer security texts concentrate not on the question of locating a perpetrator, but rather on keeping them out in the first place; it is also one of the most important reasons why there have been relatively few prosecutions.

Of course, in some cases it might not in fact be necessary even to perform these traces. In an interesting recent case in the UK, an injunction was served via electronic mail to an anonymous individual whose Internet address was known. This occurred in April 1996, and was performed by the UK solicitors firm Schilling and Lom, who had received an anonymous e-mail message threatening to publish libellous material about one of their clients [Locket 1996]. Having obtained an injunction against the anonymous publisher, the solicitor involved was able to persuade a judge to allow the document to be served over a return e-mail message. Of course, injunctions in the 'real-world' must be presented to the person concerned – or if posted, must be acknowledged.

Key to the success of this serving of an injunction therefore was the acknowledgement by the anonymous recipient of the e-mail containing the document. In fact, he or she sent back an abusive and offensive rejoinder to the injunction – but that was deemed sufficient acknowledgement! Thereafter, breaking the injunction would put the anonymous publisher in contempt of a UK court – although quite what steps could be taken are far from clear. As with many other aspects of cyberspace, this issue is a confusing and rapidly evolving one.

In this case, the offending individual, although not a 'hacker', was found to be overseas, in mainland Europe. This could equally be the case when and if connections to a specific hacker can be traced – and unlike the anonymous publisher, the hacker might well not be content simply to acknowledge the injunction. It therefore becomes necessary to track the individual – rather than the uid – in person. This, however, gives rise to a third problem, that of *jurisdiction*.

Jurisdiction in cyberspace

Although it would appear to be so, cyberspace is not a domain that lies strictly outside of the real-world legal jurisdictions.

Computer users, host systems, network connections and database resources all lie within some country – they are all therefore covered by the jurisdiction of some country's law enforcement agencies. There are two elements to the jurisdiction problems surrounding cyberspace, however. The first is the question of which country has responsibility for pursuing a crime; the second is the police force or agency that should be involved.

Neither of these questions is as straightforward as the case in the real world, with more mundane crimes. In the UK, for example, a crime in Leeds is investigated and prosecuted within Leeds; and a crime that involves, say, tax evasion is pursued by the Inland Revenue. In the case of many computer crimes, it is not always obvious which of the several authorities should be investigating the offence – and even if it can be determined as, say, a police matter, it is not always obvious which police force has responsibility.[119]

When the offence goes beyond national boundaries, this becomes more complex still. Where the offence goes beyond, say, US individual state boundaries, it becomes a federal interest crime – in the case of computer fraud and abuse, it will be investigated mainly by the Secret Service (as the US Treasury's investigative arm) or by the FBI, Air Force OSI, etc.

Within the European Union, by contrast, cross-border investigations are supported by means of mutual cooperation – so-called Mutual Legal Assistance Treaties exist between member states, so that each will undertake investigations within their own countries on behalf of the others; there is, however, no equivalent of a *federal* investigative body within the European Commission. There is 'Interpol', but this serves to coordinate cross-border investigations, rather than to perform them directly itself.

Therefore, where the crimes lie within existing and established legal boundaries – either entirely within particular states, or within wider associations, there is a mechanism to handle them. Outside of these cases, there are a series of specific relationships between individual countries – between the UK and US, for example – that would allow the pursuit of those hackers. In other cases, however, there is no such relationship, and the legal issues involved are very difficult.

This is a problem that is not unique to the crimes of computer misuse: drugs, pornography and arms can all involve such cross border activity. However, the purely technical aspects of computer misuse make it particularly difficult for the police or investigators to comprehend; when taken in conjunction with these jurisdictional problems, it becomes more difficult still.

Interestingly, however, the issue of global jurisdiction can – and indeed, has – worked to the prosecution's advantage in certain cases. For example, recall the discussion in Chapter 4 about the US situation with respect to First Amendment protection of pornography: material that would not be considered 'obscene' under the Miller test in California might well be so under the same test in another state; California is notoriously permissive, and the Miller test includes consideration of 'community standards'.

An interesting element of US law – established in a 1979 ruling – is that the government can choose the community whose standards have been offended in the case where allegedly obscene material is passed between communities (which need not be entire states) having different standards of obscenity [Cavazos 1994]. As a result, a Californian BBS operator was recently extradited to Tennessee by the FBI, on the basis that the prosecution would be (and indeed, was) successful there; it was simply necessary for them to find an Arkansas resident who had witnessed the contents of the BBS, and found them offensive [Smith 1996].

This can, of course, be argued as 'fair game': if the hackers, pornographers and others are prepared to use the globality of the medium to *their* advantage, so too should the authorities – and in a later section we will consider the directions in which this could proceed.

Detecting, tracking, locating and arresting computer hackers is therefore particularly problematic – although as we shall see, it has been done. In all such cases to date, the remote hackers have indeed been located within countries that are 'reachable' from the offended country: in the case of Stoll's German spies, the US and (then West) German authorities worked closely – albeit with some difficulties; and in the hunt for Mitnick, the search proceeded throughout the mainland US. It *is* possible to conceive of developments in which such searches become physically or geographically impossible, but to date this has not been seen.

Where the hunt is successful, however, the police's job has only just begun: it is then necessary to prosecute the hackers – an issue that relies heavily on the issue of computer-sourced forensic evidence.

COMPUTER FORENSICS

As computers become ever more involved in our everyday lives, and in the activities of criminals, it is inevitable that they will contain key evidence for very many cases. Growing numbers of fraud cases rely on the use of computers – either to direct the activity, or to hold the records. As paper-based accountancy methods are gradually supplanted by computer records, the ability to obtain evidence from the medium becomes ever more important.

There are, however, a set of very specific problems that investigators need to address in obtaining this evidence. Firstly, there is the question of actually *seizing* the evidence in the first place. That is, what powers and by what mechanisms are the police or other investigators actually empowered to seize evidence, and what are the practical implications – and even limitations – on such seizure? And secondly, there is the related aspect of ensuring that the material seized can indeed be used as evidence in the event of a prosecution.

In the case of paper records – or even, more traditional forensic evidence such as fingerprints or blood samples – this is reasonably straightforward. In 'raiding' premises, the police can seize documents within filing cabinets, bodily removing them in secure evidence bags, and if correctly handled, can then present them in court. For computer evidence, each of the simple seizure steps becomes a potential problem – both under US and UK law.

Seizing computer evidence

In 'Operation Sundevil' (the 'hacker crackdown' of 1990/1991) in the US, and within the UK in 'Operation Starburst' for example, the vast majority of seizure operations were straightforward. Police officers or Secret Service agents enacted the classic 'dawn raids', bursting into private houses through every available door – rapidly and without incident securing the individuals, premises and then the targeted material in well rehearsed, familiar procedures. In each case, the raid was supported by the serving of appropriate search and arrest warrants, and the raiding officers were well briefed on the targets for the seizure itself.

The actual protocol followed in the procedures for such seizures has been well developed – by the Secret Service and the FBI in America, and by the Serious Fraud Office in the UK. Equipment is photographed *in situ*, particularly the cabling and connections to each machine; officers then ensure that any active devices are powered down in a clean manner – if necessary, taking instructions from the owner (who in most cases is the target of the raid) but not letting them touch anything; finally, every item of equipment, print-out, storage media and other relevant items are then securely bagged and removed by the officers.

It is important to understand *why* the police or other investigators would wish to seize evidence from a computer. Firstly, the computer could be the 'victim' of the crime – suffering from a hacker raid, for example; or secondly, the computer could be being used to store illegal material – either with or without the computer owner's knowledge. In both cases, important evidence will be available within the computer – records of the illicit access, or files containing the sought-for data.

In these situations, however, the raiding officers have to be aware of further, purely *technical* aspects of seizing this evidence from the computers. Quite apart from the legal aspects, it is easily possible for a police officer – or even, more usually, the operator and owner of the computer – unwittingly to damage the evidence it contains. Taking the specific example of a hacking raid, this might have been undertaken to obtain information from the system – the hacker will therefore have accessed certain files, and it is likely that the 'last access time' on the files will show when this occurred. An investigator or operator who subsequently opens those files, a natural reaction perhaps to check that they are still intact, will then damage this evidence.

Faced with a dead body, police and the general public know not to touch anything; faced with a computer, even the police officers all too often succumb to the temptation to 'poke around'. Perversely, the most damage is performed by the victim of the hacking raid, simply looking to see what has happened; the next worse damage, however, is from those officers who are 'computer literate', but not expertly trained.

Even the directions in the evidence protocols – suggesting that machines are 'powered off' – might in fact damage evidence: a hacker could easily insert code to delete certain files during the powerdown procedure; or more importantly, processes that are still running in memory (say, viruses) will simply disappear. In the case of PCs, powering the machine down is the only option; however, UNIX and other multi-user systems also have a very useful facility called 'halt', that simply freezes the processor – thereby allowing it to be examined in due course.

In the majority of situations, however, the basic protocol is entirely effective. In some cases, officers might be accused of being overzealous – for instance, in some of the 'hacker crackdown' raids, family telephones and apparently entirely unrelated elements of electrical equipment were removed; and in the UK, there have been (no doubt apocryphal) reports of police officers seizing TV sets and even microwave ovens! Experience shows, however, that it is better to be thorough in these cases: printers, for example, contain data memory, in which illicit information can easily be stored.

Where the target of the raids is an individual, usually at his or her home, this simple approach to raid and seizure is therefore entirely appropriate and very effective. Hackers and paedophiles in particular are used to dealing with people and problems by means of remote connections; suddenly to be faced by a veritable army of (in the US, gun carrying) officers is usually sufficient to persuade total – indeed, often *abject* – cooperation.

However, in a growing number of cases, this simple situation does not apply, and more complications can ensue.

The first level of complication would be in the actual *location* of the material itself. With global Internet connections, it is entirely feasible for a paedophile to store the material within somebody else's computer – even for this to be overseas. In this case, simply seizing the local PC and disks would not provide the complete material. However, this is not the clear-cut situation it might appear. Internet connections – particularly through browsers such as Netscape – maintain a 'cache' of accessed material; this cache might well be found to contain illicit or illegal images.

Alternatively, a record of the connections themselves might also be maintained – again, allowing the material to be tracked. Producing it in evidence (considered below) might be more difficult, but finding it would not. The police could even – if this was suspected or identified as part of pre-raid intelligence work – install and use telephone or network monitoring systems to intercept the illicit traffic.

Of course, it would be possible for a suspicious or nervous paedophile to mask this element of their computer use completely. In a UK paedophile raid, for example, the seized PC was found to be entirely clean – that is, the main disk drive contained no incriminating evidence: it had been thoroughly 'sanitised' and the offending files removed. Unfortunately, the paedophile had not only deleted them but – knowing that simple deletion is not enough entirely to remove the file – had reformatted the disk and reinstalled a clean operating system on it. Suspicious of such a pristine system, the officers searched further, and found a second, hidden main disk drive that *did* contain the illegal files.

These technical challenges and difficulties are only now being appreciated in the world of law enforcement. Most worryingly, however, the legal – or even cultural – challenges are also only just beginning to become widely recognised. For example, the more complex problems in evidence seizure arise when the target of a raid is a company or establishment having a multi-user computer system. Here, while it is still possible to seize the entire computer, media and equipment, it is far from practical – and might even prove to be illegal.

In the Church of Scientology situation mentioned in Chapter 4 (page 107), for example, the ruling went against the church primarily because of the seizure method used. Perhaps the best known such situation, however, arose within the 'hacker crackdown', with the seizure of a BBS run on equipment belonging to Steve Jackson Games, a US adventure game publishers.

Steve Jackson Games

A primary target of the US Secret Service during the 1990 hacker crackdown raids was a group of hackers and phreakers called the 'Legion of Doom'. An alleged member of this gang – Craig Neidorf – was found to have copied a 'sensitive' telecommunications document describing the organisation and structure of the 'Emergency 911' system operated throughout the US.

The prosecution of Neidorf, and the near-hysterical hunt for the apparently highly valuable document, is possibly the near-lowest nadir for the Secret Service and telecommunications security personnel involved in Operation Sundevil and related investigations. The value of the document was found to have been so grossly overstated as to be laughable: initially valued at some $80 000, it was found in fact only to be worth $13! Worse still, it was found already to be in the public domain, having being published in telecommunications journals, and offered for sale through AT&T catalogues.[120]

The absolute nadir for those involved, however, came with the Secret Service's raid against Steve Jackson Games, a small, specialist publishing house in Austin, Texas. The games it published were in the form of books or manuals for so-called 'adventure' games – non-computerised, fantasy games similar to the once popular 'Dungeons and Dragons'. These were a particular favourite of many members of the Legion of Doom, and so a BBS run by Steve Jackson Games was popular with the hackers – as well as with the other, legitimate users of the games.

Unfortunately, the document stolen by Neidorf was believed to have been put on this BBS by a Steve Jackson Games employee who had previously claimed membership of the Legion. In fact, the document was *not* on the system – but nonetheless, under a sealed warrant[121] the Secret Service raided the company in March 1990. They seized and removed the BBS computer, along with the private e-mail and other, entirely legitimate data items belonging to the BBS users. They also seized all further computer equipment and 'relevant' material – as per the evidence protocol successfully applied in the case of raids against individual hackers.

Unfortunately, in performing this raid, the Secret Service effectively closed down not only the BBS – which was found to be 'clean' – but also Steve Jackson Games itself, that was unable to proceed with its legitimate business. Supported by the then newly-founded Electronic Frontier Foundation (EFF)[122] and several of the BBS users, Steve Jackson filed suit against the Secret Service – and in January 1993 was successful.

The judge found that the Secret Service had not acted within the constraints of the warrant they had had issued, particularly since the seized BBS, had not in fact held the E911 document that was the supposed object of the search. More damaging, their actions had actually been positively illegal, in that their 'interception' of the BBS users' private e-mail was against the Electronic Communications Privacy Act and the Privacy Protection Act (described in Chapter 4).[123]

As a result of these rulings, Steve Jackson Games were awarded $50 000 in damages. The damage to the Secret Service's reputation – and indeed, to the simple seizure protocol for computer evidence – was immense. As a result, certainly within the UK the SFO's computer evidence protocol now includes directions for on-site collection of computer records through cooperation with the company involved, rather than seizure of entire computer units.

For such on-site recording to be practical, however, the protocol must also include directions for ensuring that the evidence obtained cannot be challenged; that is, it must be possible to maintain the integrity of the evidential material.

Computer evidence

As we have discussed, computer records will be increasingly required as evidence of criminal activities. Files containing paedophile material, audit logs indicating hacking attempts, bank account details, and even the output from artificial intelligence systems – all of these and many more will become increasingly common items. However, to be so used, it is vital that the evidence is collected and maintained appropriately. This is because, unlike the majority of other, physical evidence, digital records can be easily changed – and this alteration can be made in an invisible (or even accidental) manner.

For example, growing numbers of traffic-speed monitors now feature digital cameras.[124] The picture is not made onto and stored as a 'wet film' photograph, but rather as a digital picture encoding. However, software to manipulate these images is cheap and widespread. The problem is not that the police *will* or even *might* manipulate it – in fact, it is the most unlikely thing for them to do; however, it is very difficult for them to prove that they did *not* do such a manipulation.

Clearly, when evidence is taken from a computer, common sense therefore dictates that multiple copies be obtained – stored within a permanent and unchangeable medium such as a CD-ROM or laser disk – and that one copy is retained by the defence team involved. However, difficulties can still arise in actually *making* the copy and ensuring its evidential properties.

In making and working with the computer data, it is clearly necessary for the police or other investigators to have access to equipment that is appropriate. Unfortunately, computer technology is both expensive and rapidly changing; it is a physical – and a financial – impossibility for the investigators to keep pace with these changes. In many situations, this leads to a requirement for the police to work closely with other agencies, and even with the manufacturers of the equipment themselves.

Quite apart from this practical aspect, there is then the issue of integrity and admissibility of evidence itself. There are two main cases in which evidence must be considered in English law, and within each there are two categories of evidence relevant to computer records [CCTA 1996]. Firstly, the case can be a *criminal* or a *civil* one; and secondly, the evidence can be *real* or *hearsay*.

The distinction between criminal and civil is important with respect to the question of 'proof' – and to the evidence law that is to be applied. In criminal cases, the 1984 Police and Criminal Evidence Act is applied; and for civil, the new 1995 Civil Evidence Act. In criminal cases, the burden of proof is generally much greater, and it should be given the greater punishments – particularly those that are custodial – that might be applied. In civil cases, the standard of proof is 'balance of probabilities' – in criminal it might be 'beyond reasonable doubt', for example. The major distinction between the two cases in English law, however, is with regard to the issue of 'hearsay'.

Computer records that are produced entirely automatically, as a result of the normal operation of a digital machine, are considered to be 'real' evidence – that is, they can be relied upon, provided that the investigators have taken appropriate steps to confirm that the computer was indeed operating normally at the time the evidence was seized. In simple terms, 'real' evidence is data which does not originate within a human mind. Because of this, elements such as dates, times and process information written automatically into an audit log would be acceptable as evidence, provided of course that they have not been subsequently manipulated, edited or in any way altered.

The automatic generation of evidential data by a computer is, unfortunately, by far the least interesting such case. In most situations – since obviously it is a *human* on trial, not a computer – the data will have originated in a human mind – and thus the issue of hearsay evidence is important. Where the computer data has been shown to have been entered by the defendant, it is admissible as 'real' – so, if the defendant has admitted typing a relevant document, this can be used as evidence. In all other cases, however, the data will have resulted from a non-automatic process initiated or controlled by another individual – evidence of this nature is hearsay, and is admissible only under a set of special circumstances.

In civil cases, the new act allows hearsay evidence to be admitted in most situations, but stresses that the weight that the judge gives to the evidence must be carefully determined, depending on the way in which the computer record has been produced. Rather than imposing special restrictions, this new law therefore provides broad discretion to the judge involved.

Because the act is so new, there has not yet been established a body of case law from which its application can be assessed. It is, however, much simpler than the situation implicit in the older, 1968 Civil Evidence Act, in which a set of more complex conditions had to be met before computer records could be admitted. These not only required the computer to have been operating correctly, but that also it should have been storing or processing information similar to that which is to be admitted. Of course, it is difficult to assess whether the computer was indeed 'working properly': does this encompass, for instance, the situation in which a hacker has penetrated its defences?

By contrast, in the case of criminal prosecutions, there is a well-established set of guidelines controlling the admissibility of computer records, even when hearsay. Section 69 of PACE allows a computer record to be admitted as evidence only when there are no reasonable grounds to believe the record to be inaccurate due to improper use of the computer, and that the computer was (again) operating properly – or that if not, the improper operation was not such as to affect the record itself.[125]

This is a simpler set of conditions than were in force in the 1968 act – but even with PACE and the new civil evidence act, it is still essential to establish the proper working of the system, and the seizure of evidence in a controlled manner. For this reason, it is often essential to introduce 'expert witnesses' into the proceedings to testify that the submitted record is indeed trustworthy. In effect, the weight of evidence is then determined by the court's trust in the *expert* rather than in the data records themselves.

Despite these problems, growing experience within the judiciary is leading to a greater acceptance of such evidence, and to an increasing reliance upon it. This is seen to be even more important as the courts themselves begin to rely upon computers – for trials, submission of evidence, and even for their management.

WIRED COURTROOMS

The final areas within which digital technology in general can be used by the judiciary lie within the courts themselves. Like any 'business' in the information age, courts rely on the manipulation and processing of information: cases must be scheduled, paperwork produced and disseminated, and information from a wide variety of third parties must be brought together. We can therefore see several aspects of courts' day-to-day activity that can benefit from the now widespread introduction of computers, telecommunications and sophisticated software:

■ Judges in both civil and criminal cases are being encouraged to rely increasingly on the use of laptops or other PCs – from writing notes, through e-mail communications, to the scheduling of their own case loads. Indeed, Lord Justice Woolf's study of the civil judicial system [Woolf 1996] placed a great emphasis on this use of technology by the judges themselves. Project JUDITH, for example, was established in 1992 by the then Lord Chancellor's Department with the plan to provide adequate technology[126] to all of the now Court Service's judges.

■ A growing number of CD-ROMs and other media – such as the Internet – now provide access to on-line legal resources. These have been available for many years to lawyers or the professions but are now increasingly available to the public. Along with these information sources, however, there are also a growing number of usable front-end systems that allow an untrained public to access comprehensive and comprehensible legal advice without huge expense. This could revolutionise the way in which the public receive such advice [Susskind 1996] – and radically alter the balance of legal power and accessibility of the courts.

■ Computers can be used increasingly within the courts to gain access to appropriate records without the administrative overhead and time delay associated with the present system. In the UK, the unit responsible for the Coordination of the Computerisation of the Criminal Justice System (the CCCJS) have run pilot projects throughout 1995 – for example, one such was to introduce more streamlined production of records via electronic media to the Reading Magistrates' Court. In place of the four-week turnaround for paper records from the DVLA at Swansea, Reading can now access relevant records in just 20 minutes [Hayward 1995].

■ Computer systems are being used increasingly to record the proceedings in court, with stenographers entering data directly into a computer, from which it is displayed – effectively in real time – on a judge's screen. The system even allows the judge to annotate the material directly, thereby saving significant time within court.

■ Information age technology has already gained widespread use to support the submission of evidence, particularly video evidence from children involved in sexual abuse cases. In this, a child – or other vulnerable witness – need not enter the courtroom, but rather can be connected by means of a video link – perhaps seen only by the judge and jury – and need not in fact see (or worse, be intimidated by) the accused. Alternatively, the accused – if there is a real threat to their safety, or a risk of escape – could even stand trial over a video link.

Other witnesses can also make use of such technology. In Australia, for example, rather than require witnesses to fly thousands of miles, at great expense, video links from nearby courts are used, allowing the witness to be interviewed with far less expense or disruption.

Each of these very real prospects forms a part of the current judicial system throughout the UK. Similar measures have been introduced in US courts, in which TV cameras and other recording devices have long featured anyway. However, the prospects for digital, cyberspace technology in courts can go well beyond these simple examples.[127] Data visualisation techniques, for instance, can be used to present complex evidence in a more understandable manner; virtual reality or computer models can be used to provide 'walk throughs' of murder scenes;[128] perhaps even whole courts could sit in a virtual reality, cyberspace courtroom – but we are many years from this!

SUMMARY – PROSECUTION IN THE INFORMATION AGE

As we have seen, computer technology presents both a fundamental challenge and an exciting opportunity to the judicial systems throughout the world.

The problems that must be faced range from the technical issues of detecting whether or not a crime has indeed occurred, to the complex issue of gathering and presenting evidence – but as ever more crimes become increasingly computerised in nature, the growing use and familiarity of computers will make this a vital element of police, court and lawyers' activities.

Computers can streamline the operation of the courts themselves, and can assist the police or other investigators to comprehend crimes and apprehend the criminals responsible. Although the technology therefore presents certain difficult challenges, the judiciary cannot afford to ignore it.

Throughout the world, there are therefore attempts not simply to ensure that real-world laws are framed in such a way as to apply to the citizens of the Cybernation, but also that they can be *used* in practice.

However, just as the legal system has not remained static when faced with digital threats, nor has the threat itself – in particular, digital crimes can be seen to have evolved in a particularly worrying direction.

6

From digital crime to digital conflict

Throughout this book, we have described the ways in which digital crimes have developed, and the ways in which the judiciary, police and other investigators have been forced to respond: by the establishment of formal and explicit laws; by the application of sophisticated prevention and detection technology; and by the introduction of computer systems within the courts themselves.

The purely *criminal* aspects of illicit computer activities are difficult to control, but they have at least certain features that make them accessible to the investigators. The culprits are either organised gangs of criminals looking to steal or extort money (that can be tracked by the investigators); or they are individuals or gangs of essentially young vandals, who are often all too willing to confess (even to *boast*) about their activities when caught.[129]

By contrast with this 'simple' situation, as the ability to perform digital mayhem progresses, it is all too likely that it will become the domain not simply of the criminal, but of organised, politically-motivated, military action – either on the part of subversive pressure groups, of terrorists, or of the armed forces themselves. This final chapter takes us far from the original worries of student hackers and mischievous viruses, into the domain of well-planned, well-managed bloodshed; from technological curiosity to armed conflict.

CYBERWAR

The Director of Information Warfare at the US Department of Defense, Emmet Paige, defines 'Information Warfare' as follows [Power 1995]:

> Information Warfare consists of actions taken to achieve inform-ation superiority in support of national military strategy by affecting adversary information and information systems while leveraging and protecting our information and information systems. ... Information Warfare addresses the opportunities and vulnerabilities inherent in increasing dependency on information and the use of information throughout the conflict spectrum. ... Information Warfare has offensive and defensive elements. ...

The important elements of this definition are the requirement that such warfare activities are performed in support of 'national mili-tary strategy', that it involves both 'offensive and defensive elements', and that it is important 'throughout the conflict spec-trum'. Information warfare will become as central to battles of the future as 'firepower', 'air superiority' and 'mobility' have proved to be in the battles of this century.

Throughout the 1990s, the concept of waging war primarily through the manipulation, subversion or damage of an enemy's information processing capabilities has grown in relevance. In 1993, the then Chairman of the US Joint Chiefs of Staff, General Colin Powell, instructed that both Information and C2 warfare (discussed below) be integrated into the US battle planning process.

The central importance of *information* in the management of warfare is well established – from the aphorisms of Sun Tzu, through the deliberately planned deceptions of the Mongol hordes and the Enigma code-breakers of World War II, to the focused and well-managed activities of the allies in the Gulf war or even of the NATO forces in the Bosnian conflict [Haeni 1995]. However, it is only recently that the full potential for targeted 'hacker' or virus activities in the domain of strategic, global conflict has been recognised outside of the realm of science fiction.

Cyberwar is the nightmare extreme of the civilian hacking activity – but it is a very real prospect that the judiciary, police and military planners cannot afford to ignore. Equally, it is a very real *opportunity* that must be grasped. To many in the military and security organisations in both the UK and the US, this threat or potential is little more than a fantasy – but just as the police and other investigators have had to learn about and use cyberspace, even the most recalcitrant of the armed forces will have to learn to *fight* there – either to protect their country from such an attack, or to benefit from the ability to use the medium themselves.

For example, during the build-up to the Gulf war, a convicted hacker took part in a US Air Force OSI ('Office of Special Investigations') experiment at Bolling Air Force Base. Over a period of three weeks, the hacker was observed breaking security at over 200 air force systems – not one reported the fact [Warren 1996].

And in September 1995, a US navy exercise to test computer security was undertaken. In an unannounced hacker attack, an air force captain (using equipment purchased from a local store, and accessing via an Internet service provider's local node) succeeded in penetrating the security surrounding a warship computer system, while the ship was at sea – successfully gaining control of its command systems, and from them of a whole battle group.[130]

The ease with which such supposedly well-secured systems could be penetrated was a bitter pill for the navy to swallow, but as the US House Speaker Newt Gingrich said in November 1995 in the context of Cyberwar: 'We had better be prepared for zones of creativity in our opponents we've never dreamed of.' And US Vice-Admiral Cebrowski, the commander of the Pentagon's systems, expressed the new and growing concern among US military planners very succinctly: 'There is no national sanctuary from information attack.'[131] The issue of 'national sanctuary' is one to which we will return in due course.

The names given to this type of conflict vary greatly: 'Cyberwar' – the term we will use here; 'Information Warfare' – a synonym and the term preferred by the US Department of Defense; 'Hacker

War' – seen as a specific subset of the Cyberwar tactics[132] discussed below; and 'Command and Control Warfare' – a 'limited option' aspect of full Cyberwarfare, involving those computer systems that direct primarily military systems in tactical situations.

The distinction between *Cyberwar* and *Command and Control Warfare* (dubbed C2 Warfare)[133] is an important one to make. In the latter case, the object of the digital attack is the purely *military* computer systems responsible for directing the tactical response of battlefield units. The systems which direct and control fighter aircraft deployment; the control systems for warships; the tactical data network linking armoured or artillery units – all of these are the legitimate targets of C2 assaults.

C2 warfare is performed therefore against military, operational targets – particularly during the tactical or field operational elements of a battle plan; it might therefore be ordered and coordinated by the brigade, battalion or even company command-level officers. In 'traditional' patterns of warfare, it might involve directed bombing campaigns against known radio sites – or even against those vehicles carrying more than the usual number of aerials.

By contrast, the full Cyberwar is performed against national, strategic targets – and would be ordered and coordinated from the highest, executive level: higher than divisional, and probably higher even than Commander-in-Chief levels. Because the targets of Cyberwar are not operational battlefield elements of the usual kind, but rather the digital infrastructure on which a *country* depends, the responsibility for any such attack belongs at the highest levels of military and political authority.

In the main, Cyberwar has been considered in the context of 'national military strategy' – that is, an activity performed by or directed at the country's armed forces. It is important to realise, however, that such weaponry and tactics are available not simply to countries fighting one another, but also to terrorist organisations, to pressure groups – and to individuals 'fighting' against national governments, big business or even 'objectionable' lobby groups.

This 'Digital Terrorism' is addressed below, but it is easy to see how C2 warfare can drift inexorably to full Cyberwar. A military dependence upon the security of computerised command and control systems is of course patently obvious – as is the need for the protection which the military would wish to extend to those systems; a corporate and individual dependence on computer technology is now also increasingly obvious. But equally, because of this corporate dependence, our nation states themselves also have a dependence upon the digital technology.

A telecommunications infrastructure, connecting computers throughout the world, supports the control of aeroplanes, trains, and traffic lights; it coordinates electricity generation and the flow of sewage; and it manages the distribution of funds between banks, etc, etc. In warfare, these roads, banks, dams and power stations are obvious targets for offensive actions: bombing by aeroplanes, missiles or by small teams of commandos. In Cyberwar, these facilities are equally well-recognised targets, but are 'bombed' through digital means (discussed below). This is a very attractive proposition to digital terrorists with the minimum of resources – or to foreign powers unable to strike at US or European governments through any other means.

On the one hand, this might be seen as a 'civilised' development of warfare and terrorism: when a logic bomb 'explodes', there is no flying shrapnel, no burning buildings or shattered limbs. However, the damage from a logic bomb is no less severe, and might in fact be much less apparent – but it too can cause death or injury: if computer systems on railways are caused to fail then trains crash and kill people as easily as would a missile attack – and with perhaps far greater accuracy and effect.

In many ways, this is ironic; the Internet in particular was developed to ensure that the US military communications could survive and work around the damage resulting from a nuclear attack. That the Internet itself could host a more insidious attack against those very institutions, or more worryingly against a national infrastructure, is a suprising, science fictional development. Indeed, this very feature has been taken sufficiently seriously that it has become a part of the US and other countries' battle planning concerns: in 1995 the US Navy, for example, established a 'Fleet Information Warfare Centre' dedicated to attacking or denying an opponent's access to vital information, telecommunication or computing resources; the US air force and marine corps have similar facilities. Science fiction that has become chilling reality.

Offensive manipulation of information and of information processing resources can be seen to have three potential elements:

1 The activity is essentially personal: individual or small groups of hackers direct their own activities, aimed at satisfying their own immediate, non-strategic ends.
2 This activity is performed by or on behalf of companies – with the equivalent of high-technology industrial espionage.
3 The conflict moves on to a global, politically directed and motivated stage, with activities featuring as a single, tactical element of a more widely coordinated, strategic offensive.

At present, the activities in these areas – other than the first – is not readily apparent. There have been claims of such espionage, including reports in August 1996 accusing the American CIA of hacking into and abstracting trade negotiation material from a European Commission computer network.[134] There have also been widespread claims of related industrial espionage, featuring offensive computer manipulation – but at present, the outright warfare aspects are (thankfully) absent; despite this, a variety of organisations throughout the world are examining the potential – and the planned response – that it implies.

At least in part, this activity is motivated by the very real fear that a series of computer calamities in the early 1990s induced in the US authorities. The most spectacular of these problems was in September 1991, when the simultaneous failure of several telephone switching systems in New York City cut the voice and data communication services to the city's airports. No less than 85 000 passengers were stranded, unable to call home or make fresh travel arrangements; over 500 flights were cancelled; and all activity at Kennedy, La Guardia and Newark airports came to a halt.

Investigations of this and of the several other similar problems that beset AT&T in 1990 and 1991 showed that the service interruptions were not, as originally thought, the activity of phreakers – or worse, of terrorist-motivated hackers. Rather, software bugs and human errors in system maintenance were to blame.[135] Nonetheless, the response to the problems was threefold: a legal clampdown on the activities of hackers in the US, leading to several arrests, 'showtrials' and the seizure of equipment; a heightened media attention on the issues and risks surrounding the penetration of strategic or infrastructural computing resources; and the establishment of several studies and position papers from the US military, colleges and security organisations[136] proposing strategies to address a newly perceived, national threat.

THE TACTICS AND WEAPONS OF CYBERWARFARE

As the definition quoted above said, Information Warfare covers the whole 'conflict spectrum'. In terms of specific conflict activities, there are five areas of particular interest: intelligence, disinformation, denial, destruction and protection. Before we consider for *whom* the digital, techno-warrior might be fighting, we will first look at the detailed activities that each of these activities imply – and indeed *how* the warrior actually fights, and with what weapons [Magsig 1995].

Intelligence

In military terms, 'Intelligence' involves *discovering* the enemy's position and what one's enemy might know or be involved in doing; *deducing* what actions the enemy's knowledge might lead or point towards; and *deciding* what responses the enemy might make to any of the potential initiatives that one's own side might launch. In the Cyberwar context, this therefore involves the application of sophisticated digital technology to achieve these ends.

Electronic intelligence and human intelligence – in US military parlance 'Elint' and 'Humint' – have featured highly in films, books and the imagination of many Internet newsgroup contributors. That spies and spy planes (or submarines, satellites and listening posts) gather intelligence by 'listening' to the radio broadcasts of foreign countries' military installations is undeniable[137]: of course they do it. In the Cyberwar context, however, intelligence gathering can go beyond this – 'snooping' the content of an enemy's computer systems directly.

At the most obvious, hackers able to access computer systems undetected can silently, invisibly abstract huge quantities of information – indeed, the hacker that Clifford Stoll pursued in the mid-1980s was doing just that. As these computer systems have become increasingly more protected, less invasive intelligence gathering from computers has become important. This can range from passive detection of 'Van Eck Radiation' from PC or terminal screens, through the snooping of network packets, to more extreme actions such as the introduction of 'Key-Press' viruses [infiNity 1996].

Van Eck radiation is a particularly well-popularised option for such 'snooping'. All screens – just like televisions – work by means of a scanning beam of electrons fired at a fluorescing surface. When the beam is on, the screen is excited and glows at a specific dot; when the beam is off, the dot remains dark. In this way, the patterns of letters, colour and shade are produced. However, whenever the beam is switched on, a burst of very low energy radiation is emitted: 'Van Eck' radiation.

Suitably sensitive radio detectors can receive this emission, and with sufficiently powerful signal processors an eavesdropper can therefore monitor and record the signal. This allows – in principle at least – the actual contents of the screen to be seen remotely. In practice, of course, this is not that straightforward: the signals are so faint that the detector must be very close if it is to pick up anything at all, meaning that the 'agent' is likely to be found.

Alternatively, a detector can be 'planted' alongside (perhaps even within) the terminal, but this leads to the problem of collecting the captured data. And of course, the snooping agent has no control over what is displayed, making the method a bit 'hit or miss'. Worst of all – from the agent's perspective – the radiation is widely known about, and easily shielded. The military in fact insist on such equipment having been 'Tempest' proofed – ie, shielded from radiating 'transient electro-magnetic pulse emanations' – by the simple expedient of a surrounding metal grill.

Despite the difficulties of detecting such signals, and the ease with which they can be shielded, so-called 'Tempest attacks' are a widely popularised form of Cyberwar – at least within Internet newsgroups. A fair-minded analysis of the prospect would have to conclude that the low quality of intelligence that could be so gathered (ie, even passwords – that are never displayed – would be unavailable) in conjunction with the difficulty in so gathering it makes it a very unpromising tactic.[138]

Better is the 'Key-press Virus' approach. In this, a virus infects a target PC, perhaps via hostile applet, or through 'normal' infection from diskette or Internet file. However, instead of damaging the PC or its contents, the virus simply records the first few hundred characters typed, in the expectation that these will include the password. Alternatively, the virus can deliberately wait for characters typed at a password prompt. In both cases, these characters are then transmitted, for example, by e-mail back to the virus writer – the 'agent'.

IP snooping can also collect this information, with the establishment of imitation Internet sites on the network that 'pretend' to be a given address. These therefore are able – in principle at least – to receive the packets transmitted to the real site. Of course, encryption methods can easily circumvent this trick, making the virus approach the more feasible.

This form of intelligence gathering therefore uses much the same weapons and tactics as the 'normal' hacking situation – but here, the information gathering is focused and deliberate. The intention of the snooping is to gather the data necessary to permit system penetration, and thereby to allow more precise intelligence to be discovered. As with most warfare situations, the important element is not *how* the intelligence is located, but rather *why*.

Disinformation

The most obvious reason in warfare for collecting intelligence is to allow one's response and planning to be well informed. In the Cyberwar context, the intelligence gained can also be used to frame a series of activities aimed at manipulating an enemy's own information sources – introducing misleading or 'twisted' information. This can be done to confuse an enemy's planning process – by infecting the intelligence upon which *they* rely – or perhaps to subvert the enemy's own people; it can even be used to subvert third-party bystanders, upon which either side depends.

Databases can be manipulated to change information upon which the forces' planning process is to be based – for example, to hide particular radar reports, equipment location, or unit status. This would be a very obvious, *military* action; however, far more interesting would be manipulation that acts in a subtle manner upon the 'national sanctuary'.

This issue of a sanctuary was mentioned above, and is an important concept not just in Cyberwar, but within *any* military conflict. In the case of the US in particular, national security has historically depended upon two key elements: the 'Projection of Force' into distant theatres of conflict; and the maintenance of a protected industrial base within which munitions, equipment and personnel can be developed. Not since the Civil War has the US had to fight upon its own territory.[139] Generations of soldiers, generals and politicians have therefore grown up with the belief that the 'national sanctuary' of industrial-military complex, home towns and secure command and control is proof from all but a full-scale, nuclear conflict – which is prevented by the establishment of a counter nuclear threat.

A GI on the ground therefore fights – and has for many years fought – with the belief that his home town, country and family are in a safe haven to which he will (if he is lucky) return. This need not, however, always be the case. Although the US homeland is well outside the range of all but the opposing superpowers' bombs and missiles, it *is* accessible by means of computer connections – particularly the Internet.

A viable Cyberwar target, for example, would then be the infra-structure – particularly the economic infrastructure – within this sanctuary. Consider the situation if, for instance, the soldier's bank account was deleted by a hacking attack on the part of the enemy; or worse, if his house was repossessed due to an error within the mortgage company's system. While fighting the *enemy*, he would also have to be fighting the bank, the mortgage or utility companies – that is, he would have to be fighting his *own country*. The acid which acted to erode the US GIs' confidence during the Vietnam war was caused by 'enemy sympathisers' – in a future conflict, it could be a deliberately planned activity on the part of an enemy, as fundamental to their campaign as an airstrike or artillery bombardment.[140]

Disinformation about the politicians guiding the conflict (such as morphed pictures, mentioned above), or about the enemy's intentions, or about the reaction to the conflict at home: all of these could sap an army's – or even a country's will to fight a conflict. And this carries over to conflicts which are non-geograph-ical: terrorists can (as we shall shortly discuss) use Cyberwar tactics very effectively.

Denial

Beyond the snooping and pollution of an enemy's information resources, Cyberwarfare can also involve denying the enemy access to these very resources. There is an important distinction to be made between *denial* and *destruction*. Once destroyed, the resource (whatever it might be) is unavailable to one's enemy, oneself – and perhaps most importantly, to the innocent civilian victims of a conflict, who are often then responsible for rebuilding a shattered country following a war.

By destroying sufficiently much of a telecommunications net-work to deny an enemy its access, but not destroying the infrastructure itself, it becomes possible to gain an immediate, tactical superiority – and then easily to re-establish the service following victory. This denial effect can be achieved, by example, through the introduction of an encrypting virus that effectively removes sensitive data or command programs – but allows them easily to be replaced through simply reversing the encryption, exactly as with the attacks against banks described above.

Another aspect of this involves using 'denial of service' attacks aimed at key systems during sensitive periods. For example, an 'overload' attack against a command and control system might not succeed in damaging it – or the data it holds – but it can easily succeed in 'distracting' the system long enough for some other activity to proceed. If a computer system is too busy repelling unwanted login attempts by offensive intruders to allow a legitimate operator to gain access, then the system has been subverted as effectively as if it had been physically destroyed.

Destruction

In the more usual case, the attacker will indeed wish positively to destroy key information processing or telecommunication resources. Hacking attacks followed by data removal; well-placed bombs – even attacks involving high-intensity radio fields to 'fry' the sensitive electronics within computerised systems can all be involved. This is perhaps the aspect of Cyberwar that most closely resembles the public perception of 'ordinary' digital vandalism.

An important point to recognise, however, is that such wholescale destruction of computing resources is in fact very difficult for *hackers* to achieve. True, it is possible to remove key files – but sensible working practice involves the maintenance of back-ups. True, it is possible to use HIRF guns – but the range for these is very short, requiring the attacker to be so close that they might as well simply kick the computer to destruction. An explosives attack is by far the most likely success – and this is well beyond the abilities (if not the ambitions) of most teenage hackers.

By contrast, in military or terrorist attacks, this is not only *possible*, it is entirely *practical*: missile attacks against microwave towers, switching stations, television masts and known computer centres were all a key element in the Gulf war; the military are well practised in launching such successful attacks – and already have the necessary equipment to do so. HIRF weapons, for example, were developed by the military to provide a defence against 'smart' missiles, allowing the sensitive guidance systems to be destroyed while the missile was in flight.

Protection

The ability to use such tactics offensively also, however, imposes a requirement to ensure protection from an enemy's use of the same weapons. Strong system security becomes a mandatory for the military systems – but also for the 'civilian' systems upon which the 'national sanctuary' depends.

This introduces what might well be seen as the most crucial aspect of Cyberwar: *who is vulnerable*? Given the history and experience of the US in particular, it is an almost implicit and subconscious belief that only the armed forces are at risk during an armed conflict: Vietnam, the Gulf, Bosnia – even the two World Wars were all fought many thousands of miles away from the homeland.[141]

However, in Cyberwar, the enemy can strike at the heart of this previously sacrosanct homeland. This is of course a frightening prospect – but it is in part because of the relative levels of protection: military systems are developed with high levels of security in mind; they are operated within an equally strong security requirement. By contrast, civilian systems are much more vulnerable to attack.

Perhaps more importantly, however, an attack against even well-protected civilian systems – such as the banks – can have a much greater effect than an equally successful attack against the military. The armed forces are trained to have a particular 'mind-set' – especially those who are at the front line. Equipment upon which they depend can fail at any moment, due to enemy action. Because of this, they train carefully to simulate the actions of such failure. Even the most secure of civilian systems, however, are depended upon to a crucial degree – a failure in these therefore results in a much longer and more confused operational hiatus.

Of course, there are many civilian systems that are provided with rapid and fully planned contingency services – the Stock Exchange, banks and so forth. But equally, there are many more civilian systems whose failure would lead to panic, confusion and a long-term suspension of operation. Consider the effect, for example, that a deliberately planned attack against the traffic control systems within a city centre would have, particularly if combined with an attack against police command and control systems, the emergency telephone service, and the underground control systems. While a similar attack against an operational military unit would be reacted to very quickly, the response in the civilian case would be absolute chaos.

Prevention – in the full Cyberwar case – therefore involves a careful assessment not simply of the military targets and their vulnerabilities, but also the impact that digital attacks might have on the civilian infrastructure upon which the military depend – operationally *and* emotionally. We might also remark in passing that much of computer security (as discussed particularly in Chapter 1) centres on an analysis of the *risks* faced by an organisation; by contrast, in Cyberwar it is necessary to concentrate on the *threats*. There might be a risk of fire – but a threat of arson; there might be a risk of computer failure – but a threat of hacking attacks. A 'threat' is a 'risk' that is controlled and directed – in this case, by an enemy. To face the Cyberwar challenge, it is therefore necessary to know from whom it might come.

DIGITAL TERRORISM

The 'conflict spectrum' mentioned in the definition of Information Warfare above not only encompasses the several important activities of Cyberwar, which are in fact simply the application of existing and long-established battle tactics in a novel domain. It is also necessary to consider two further aspects of the conflict spectrum: what and whom is being attacked; and who the attacker is.

Of course, there might well be situations in which two companies 'fight' each other – for market share, or for control of a particular invention. This might include elements of Cyberwar tactics – from intelligence gathering, even to destruction of a rival's computer resources. This *is* a major worry, but the threat of damage to companies is far more likely to come from terrorist groups.[142] This is not to say that companies won't 'spy' on one another – of course they will: this is part and parcel of modern corporate life; but most would draw the line at deliberately destroying even a bitter rival's property (intellectual or physical). The bad publicity, court action and damage costs likely to result would make such activity far from sensible.

In a full-scale war, by contrast, two *countries* fight one another – for territory, access to sea lanes, or even for religious reasons. The activities are therefore directed by the national governments, with stated national objectives in mind, and encompass not simply the destruction of intellectual property, but even of life. This is the type of warfare envisaged by most civilians – and even many military planners: the Gulf war, the world wars and the majority of conquest wars waged over the centuries conform to this pattern. It is, however, by no means the *only* type of warfare. In Civil wars, for example, two or more elements of a given nation fight for control of the homeland itself – perhaps even including revolution by an oppressed majority, throwing off control by a single, hated individual.

History is full of the tragic consequences of such destructive activities (laudable or despicable though the motives may have been) – but by far the most common form of conflict is now on a much smaller scale: 'Low Intensity Conflict' (LIC), embodied in guerrilla or terrorist actions – involving small, highly mobile forces able and willing to strike at 'soft' targets to generate as much concern – and indeed, *terror* – as possible within national governments and national populations.

Given the nature of Cyberwarfare and of terrorism, it is clear that by far the more dangerous perpetrators of Cyberwarfare are these small-scale forces [Richardson 1996]. This is because they are obviously eager to avoid the full-scale, fixed point battles that have formed the basis of open warfare in the classic conflicts of the past – and are content to strike against the less well guarded, civilian infrastructure, careless of the risk to life and property that such attacks imply.

Would a terrorist – or even a protest group – that doesn't balk at the use of plastic explosives in public places hesitate if given the chance to plant a computer virus in a railway control system? Undoubtedly not – and the introduction of viruses, hacking attacks and similar can be performed from many miles away, perhaps from another country, or even another continent; the ultimate in 'stand-off' weaponry.

Against whom might such digital terrorism be waged? There are three possible targets: the national government itself within a particular country; companies or particular businesses that pose a threat – or are thought to be objectionable by the terrorist; or specific social or ethnic groups.

Digital terrorism against the national infrastructure is the obvious application of Cyberwar tactics by such small, active units capable of mounting hacking, virus or more extreme attacks – indeed, this is a logical extension of the more severe combat situation outlined above. It differs only insofar as the campaign is unlikely to be directed by individuals (or indeed, national governments) against which the attacked country could react.

The second two categories of attack are, however, perhaps the more worrying. Protest activism has mounted in intensity and in violence over recent years, covering objectionable activities such as the mistreatment of or experimentation on live animals; the building of roads through forests; and the export of military technology to oppressive regimes. An obvious, logical development of such protests would be a move towards increasing use of 'remote' weapons such as computer viruses rather than baseball bats or explosives – particularly by what might be thought of as 'middle-class terrorist' groups, drawn from educated and articulate groups.[143]

As an example, Cyberwar tactics could easily allow roads protesters to access the computers of the contractors, reading or even changing works orders; they could manipulate data within the council's computers; they could even ensure that certain contractors were never paid. All of these are valid, Cyberwar tactics, likely to appeal to many of the 'softer' protest groups. Such tactics have not – at the time of writing – actually occurred, but already government departments such as the UK Treasury have expressed concern that their Internet connections might well support – or even give rise to – hacking attacks upon them in the event of unfavourable Budget receptions. Such illegal and unwelcome activities can surely only be a matter of time.

Perhaps the most worrying of the digital terrorist potentials, however, would be deliberately planned and well-directed information attacks against individuals or ethnic groups. Manipulation of sensitive data about particular people could easily allow racist groups to attack minorities in a subtle yet cruel way. Manipulation of stored data concerning immigrant families, for example, could be far more damaging – but yet, much less emotive – than physical attacks against their person. Should such attacks occur, it will be difficult in the extreme for the authorities to react to a barely understood threat, carried out for the basest of motivations.

We have seen that the weapons, delivery system and expertise required to wage a successful Cyberwar campaign are now a part of modern, everyday life. Ultra-powerful computers can be bought or leased for a tenth of the price of a family car; global Internet connections make the virus, cracking and hacking software freely available; and the Internet can equally easily allow the attack to be waged against the terrorist's chosen target from the comfort of a suburban back bedroom. Safely ensconced in one's digital anonymity, the most offensive of actions can be performed for the basest of motives, or out of love of country; and as we have seen, the Cybercops and guardsmen ranged against the attacker are barely coming to grips with the concept, let alone mounting an adequate defence.

SUMMARY – FROM DIGITAL CRIMES TO DIGITAL CONFLICT

The progression of digital crimes has been a frightening one: from the most mundane and accidental of security breaches, hacking, virus writing and elements such as computer-supported fraud have developed in sophistication and application in an almost exponential growth. From the earliest of mischievous computer penetrations, we have progressed to the point at which seemingly every computer and operating system in common use can be broken into at will. But by far the most terrifying aspect of this development has been the way in which the *directors* of such activity have evolved.

From an essentially 'fun' activity, the breaking of computer and data protection systems has become a part of any future battlefield. From reasonably simple crime, digital offences have progressed to the point of being threats to the national security of the developed countries. Warships and even satellites can be penetrated and subverted by careful application of the most mundane of equipment, from homes throughout the world.

This is *not* science fiction: it is very, very real – although it might sound to be the most outrageous of notions. Hacking, fraud and computer abuse, a problem in its current, somewhat undeveloped form, could become the scourge of the 21st century; could support the activities of terrorists, national enemies and the most extreme of pressure groups. And this is a worry that is being faced actively by organisations such as the CIA, NSA and the US Secret Service – perhaps the least excitable groups in the world.

As we move into the age of the Cybernation, it is apparent that the Internet in particular, and digital technology in general, has produced a 'Pandora's Box' of effects – a liberating technology that threatens our national, corporate and personal security; a technology that must be mastered before it masters us.

Our analysis has taken us a long way – from the most mundane of real-world thefts, through legal and judicial elements, to the offensive (in all meanings of the word) activities of the digital terrorist. A fascinating, frightening and challenging study.

Conclusion:
Policing the cybernation

Just as the highwayman of old used the primitive communication mechanism of the day – turnpike and cart-track – we should not be surprised that the age of digital technology brings its own 'Information Highway Robber'.

Where wealth is stored, processed and transported through the cyberspace connections, it is of course predictable that criminals will follow – and the legislators, regulators and police will equally be drawn. Throughout the text, we have shown the way in which these criminal activities have progressed, from the first, faltering steps of the phreakers, hackers and teenage gangs, to the professional, organised and strategic activities of the techno-warriors.

From being the playground of academics and researchers, the Internet in particular has begun the long and painful growth into a fully functional, politicised and free-standing society – the Cybernation. It attracts new members from all walks of life, from all industries, and of all ages – but equally, it has attracted the con-men, the thieves, the grifters and the vandals; and it allows the terrorist to hide, unnoticed.

Sixteen years ago, along with a small number of others, I stumbled into this cyberspace – drawn by the free-wheeling discussion groups, the heady mixture of technology, anarchy and a global platform from which to shout about what then seemed important, and now seems much less so. There were newsgroups about science fiction, hacking, computer systems, and non-linear pro-gramming languages; there were global, multi-user text-based adventure games; and there was a world-wide network of com-puter systems, information resources and *people* with which to interact.

We hacked into the network, feverishly trying to circle the globe with a tenuous, invisible string of remote login connec-tions; we left rude messages on terminals as far afield as Australia, Canada and even Hawaii; we shouted abuse at one another, secure in the privacy and protection that comes from behind the glowing VDU – we were the first settlers, playing in a new world populated up until then by the 'natives', the professional telecom-munication engineers.

The Internet of 1980 – or rather, the collection of bulletin boards, networks and DARPA connections that would grow to become '*the* Internet' – was our Greek islands: the roads were dark, rickety, unpaved and – truth to tell – slightly dangerous; there were bandits, hooligans and maniacs hiding among the rocks; but equally, there were geniuses and unimaginably vast information resources scattered throughout the islands, if you knew how to bridge from one to the next – and we did.

But now we have become victims of our own success: we shouted the praises of the cyber-islands too loudly; we provided easy ways to bridge those gaps – tools and mechanisms that drew people to the 'islands' from around the world. We have provided an environment upon which growing numbers of people rely – and which is therefore increasingly the target of concerted, directed and offensive actions. We have attracted the shops, tourists and latter-day settlers who, quite rightly, demand that the roads become safe, are paved, lit and signposted; who demand, quite rightly, that the maniacs, vandals and robbers be pursued, captured and jailed; who demand, again, quite rightly, that a community that existed for so long in a state of benign anarchy be legislated, regulated and effectively policed.

The Cybernation is not – and has never been – a free-standing community, a separate state in which the real-world of laws, regulations, police activities and even military actions do not apply. Despite appearances to the contrary, the Internet and the global association of computers and computer users occupies the physical, real world of geography, of commercial and political influences, and of legislative jurisdiction. The laws in particular might be difficult to frame, apply and act upon – but they nonetheless exist, and have a valid and important role to play in the management and exploitation of cyberspace.

To the post-modern, anarchic, cyber-punk or digital terrorist, this might seem an absurd – or worse, an irrelevant – statement; it might even seem to be a sell-out on the part of those of us who grew up with the first, faltering steps of a cyber-society – and bemoaned the commercial direction that it subsequently took. But if the Cybernation is to be *about* anything, it is about the growth of a community within a new and as yet unexplored territory, a territory that must be made safe for our children to explore and, better yet, to work and live within. A global village cannot grow and prosper if we all fear the robber, the vandal or the guerrilla at the door; if we all feel that our computers, our information and our very lives might at any moment be invaded, soiled or terrorised by the cyber-punk and his viruses.

If the World-Wide Web grants children equal access to educational and obscene images, if credit card transactions are as likely to be abused as not, and if Web pages are as likely to contain viruses as interesting information, *we will not use it* – and the Cybernation will wither and die, or worse be stifled by such draconian regulation that, like the radio waves before it, the Internet becomes simply the domain of official 'broadcasters' of authorised content; or worst of all, becomes the exclusive domain of the antisocial users.

Policing the Cybernation is a task that the authorities have only recently begun to recognise. The laws that must be applied were developed – in the main – through a hurried and often unwise response to specific threats, with often only loosely appropriate real-world analogies upon which to draw. Jurisdiction, responsibility and the application of technology to combat technological abuse all need careful consideration – a process that has begun to gather momentum.

As more and ever more people have become familiar with this cyberspace domain, inevitably some *will* prove to be crooked –

but equally inevitably, some will prove to be the good guys. It *is* true that the criminal often has greater motivation than the policeman – but the Cybercops are not the dullards that the hackers would paint them. And they are supported by technology, by business, and by governments throughout the world; but better yet, they are supported by the citizens of our Cybernation.

In the June 1996 ruling on the Exon Bill, the US judge said that the Internet 'deserves the highest protection from government intrusion'. True – but equally, it deserves the highest protection *by* the government – in the US, UK and throughout the world – if it is to meet the expectations of its users, and if it is to grow and prosper. But most importantly, it deserves the highest protection by those users.

The Internet of 1980 is now a distant but cherished memory; the Information Superhighway of 2000 is a vision – it can be the most exciting environment we have ever built, or it can be the technological equivalent of a blighted inner-city, no-go area, patrolled by vigilantes, hacker-gangs and con-men; worse still, it could be the battlefield of the future. The choice is ours.

References

Arquilla, J. and Ronfeldt, D. (1993) 'Cyberwar is coming!', *Comparative Strategy*, vol. 12, no. 2, April–June

Audit Commission (1994) 'Opportunity Makes a Thief: An Analysis of Computer Abuse', Crown Copyright

Barrett, N. (1996a) *The State of the Cybernation: Cultural, Political and Economic Implications of the Internet*, Kogan Page

Barrett, N. (1996) 'Smile, you're on Candid (digital) Camera', *Traffic Technology International*, June/July, p. 62

Bingley, L. (1995) 'Data trawling with Neural Nets', *Software Futures*, January, p. 5

Brogan, H. (1985) *The Penguin History of the United States of America*, Penguin

Castley, S. (1995) 'Changes in law on data protection and the enquiry agent', *Inside Fraud*, Autumn, p. 10

Cavazos, E. and Morin, G. (1994) *Cyberspace and the Law*, The MIT Press

CCTA (1996) 'Legal Issues and the Internet', Crown Copyright

Data Protection Registrar (1996) 'What Is Data Protection? – An Introduction to the Data Protection Act', Office of the Data Protection Registrar, March

Davis, D. (1996) 'Compliance Defects in Public-Key Cryptography', 6th USENIX Security Symposium, 29 May, p. 171

Dean, D. *et al.* (1996) 'Java Security: From HotJava to Netscape and Beyond', IEEE Symposium on Security and Privacy, 6–8 May

Economist (1996) 'The property of the mind', *The Economist* Newspaper Ltd, 17 July, p. 69

Feynman, R. (1985) *Surely You're Joking, Mr Feynman*, Counterpoint

Garfinkel, S. and Spafford, G. (1996) *Practical UNIX and Internet Security*, O'Reilly & Associates, Inc.

189

Gates, B. (1995) *The Road Ahead*, Viking

Haeni, R. (1995) 'An Introduction to Information Warfare', dissertation, George Washington University, December

Halsall, F. (1996) *Data Communications, Computer Networks and Open Systems*, Fourth edition, Addison Wesley

Heyward, D. (1995) 'The case of the vanishing paperwork', Government Computing, October, p. 12

InfiNity. (1996) 'The Feasibility of Breaking PGP', Internet URL: 'www.stack.urc.tue.nl:80', filename '/~galactus/remailers/attack-faq.html', February

Jay, R. (1996) 'Data Protection on the Internet', Office of the Data Protection Registrar, unpublished presentation, CCTA Internet & the Law Conference

LaDue, M. (1996) 'Hostile Applets on the Horizon', Internet publication URL: 'www.math.gatech.edu/~mladue/HostileArticle.html'

Lawrence, A. and Briggs, P. (1996) 'The megabit bandits', *Computer Business Review*, July, p. 9

Levy, S. (1992) *Artificial Life: The Quest for a New Creation*, Penguin

Locket, N. (996) 'Recent Developments in Internet Law', CCTA Conference 'Internet and the Law', URL 'www.barristers.co.uk/ccta.htm'

Magsig, D. (1995) 'Information Warfare in the Information Age', dissertation, George Washington University, December

Malik, I. (1996) *Computer Hacking: Detection and Protection*, Sigma Press

National Computer Centre (1996) 'The Information Security Breaches Survey 1996', DTI, ICL, ITSEC, NCC

Negroponte, N. (1995) *Being Digital*, Hodder & Stoughton

Ould, M. (1990) *Strategies for Software Engineering: The Management of Risk and Quality*, John Wiley & Sons Ltd

Power, R. (1995) 'Special Report on Information Warfare', *Computer Security Journal*, vol. 11, no. 2

Richardson, D. (1996) 'Hack attack', *Computing*, 13 June, p.38

Rich, E. (1983) *Artificial Intelligence*, McGraw Hill

Rossney, R. (1995) 'Oh look, he's brought me a present', *New Scientist*, 16 September, p. 38

Shimomura, T. (1996) *Takedown*, Secker & Warburg

Smith, G. (1996) 'Internet Law and Regulation', FT Law & Tax

Sterling, B. (1992) *The Hacker Crackdown: Law and Disorder on the Electronic Frontier*, Penguin

Stoll, C. (1991) *The Cuckoo's Egg*, Pan Books

Susskind, R. (1996) *The Future of Law*, Oxford University Press

Tabizel, D. *et al.* (1996) 'The Internet in 1996: An Investment Perspective', *Durlacher Multimedia and Intervid*, January

Tanenbaum, A. (1989) *Computer Networks*, Second edition, Prentice-Hall International Editions

Tanenbaum, A. (1992) *Modern Operating Systems*, Prentice-Hall International Editions

Thompson, K. (1984) 'Reflections on Trusting Trust', *Communications of the ACM*, vol. 27, no. 8, August

Torbet, G. *et al.* (1995) 'Vital Signs for Identification', *Computer Bulletin*, December, p. 14

Tufte, E. (1990) *Envisioning Information*, Graphics Press

Waller, D. (1995) 'Onward Cyber Soldiers', *Time Magazine*, 21 August

Warren, P. (1996) 'Criminal intelligence', *Computing*, 14 March, p. 30

Wayner, P. (1996) 'Disappearing Cryptography', *AP Professional*

Woolf, Lord Justice. (1996) 'Access to Justice', Crown Copyright

Endnotes

1. Throughout the book, particularly within these Endnotes, we have given certain details on how specific security breaches have been effected. In all cases, these are breaches that are public domain knowledge (ie, that have appeared in other publications) and that are known to have been repaired. Many other security holes still exist; and more are discovered on a constant basis – but we have not provided details on these so as not to encourage further intrusions.
2. See, for example, the relevant discussions in [Negroponte 1995] and [Gates 1995] for a more detailed over view of the types of activities and opportunities that this provides. [Barrett 1996a] gives an analysis that is more UK-centric for the Internet in particular.
3. There is nothing sinister in this latter case (although some would argue so). The road traffic monitors involve a series of sensors around junctions, which feed vehicle data to the junction control systems to ensure that the traffic lights can be responsive to changing traffic patterns; the road speed analysers (obvious on the gantries over motorways) feed data on average speeds and generate alerts when the speed drops below certain limits. This is used to inform drivers (via mobile phone-connected displays) of hold-ups in their immediate vicinity. The automated CCTV units record traffic on particular roads and are used for analysis in the case of accidents – many of them are monitored by police officers, most are simple recorders. The August/September 1996 supplement to *Traffic Technology International*, 'COMtrans' gives significant and detailed information on the operation of these systems in cities throughout the world.
4. That is, through using the so-called 'Loyalty Cards', supermarkets can record and analyse the individual spending habits and purchasing preferences of those cardholders. This allows them then

to offer targeted discounts or promotional material to those individuals, secure in the knowledge that they are not entirely inappropriate. If, for example, a regular customer is known to buy beer every week, but every week a different brand, the supermarket could promote an entirely new beer to that customer confident in the probability that they are likely to try it. A similar promotion inadvertently aimed at a non-drinker would simply waste the supermarket's money. It is the cost effectiveness of such precise targeting possibilities that help justify such applications – although in Chapter 4 we will examine the UK Data Protection principles as they apply to this case.

5. During the Gulf War, for example, a £2000-odd laptop was stolen from a British Army officer's car. The laptop contained, however, precise details of the allied campaign and strategy – the lives of hundreds of thousands of allied troops could have been lost had those details been furnished to the Iraqis.

6. A 'bulletin board system' (BBS) is a computer that supports access via telephone lines by very many people, usually using home PCs. These people can access the computer's facilities remotely, including the ability to share files between themselves, or to pass messages between them. It contrasts with the wider Internet, in that Internet access is to a world-wide network of computers – and therefore to a much wider pool of information and other users. In essence, a BBS can be controlled more effectively because it has a reasonably apparent, 'real-world' location: the central computer. The Internet is more difficult, given the diversity of systems involved. [Barrett 1996a] gives a more comprehensive and detailed assessment of the Internet's impact in the social, political and economic spheres.

7. Estimates of the Internet population vary quite dramatically. Some commentators predict as many as 500 million users by the year 2000, others that the numbers might dramatically decline as the Internet becomes saturated and even slower in its response. Regardless of the size of the population, it is readily accepted that the Internet – or the Information Superhighway as it might become – will be a key component of all organisations' infrastructure, and a significant part of all our lives [Barrett 1996a, Tabizel 1996].

8. The survey – part of a Carnegie-Mellon University research project – was skewed by the consideration of private bulletin board systems (BBSs) of an 'adult' nature. These fall outside the usual Internet concept, since they are connected to directly over telephone lines.

9. An anonymous account of the mechanisms and approaches possible for breaking one particular secure encryption method – PGP – is given in [infiNity 1996]. This is an excellent overview of the types of attack that are possible – although it is by no means certain that such attacks would work against PGP (which at the time of writing is not believed ever to have been broken).

10. So too does Netscape's Internet security system 'SSL', VISA and Mastercard's Secure Electronic Transactions scheme (SET), and indeed most of the 'automatic' encryption schemes built in to the network hardware.

11. This is a unique identifier held by the individual in the form a 'certificate'. Usually, the certificate is itself encoded by means of a simple, irreversible 'hash' algorithm, that produces a unique, single value (a large number) from the certificate contents. Nobody else need *know* therefore the certificate, only the hash result to allow unique identification to be established – this is referred to as 'Blinding'.

12. This is not to denigrate software engineering; vast strides forward have been made in the processes of specifying and correctly implementing systems. However, bridge building and other 'real-world' engineering tasks can call on centuries of experience, and on a well formulated mathematical basis. There are, of course, frequent problems with bridges or similar, but on the whole, mathematical models (or even scale models) of bridges, buildings and planes can be used with a high degree of confidence in the testing of a design. In software engineering, such a mathematical base exists, but it is very difficult to apply – each new program or system is essentially a wholly new design (otherwise it wouldn't be undertaken), even if it is formed from known and trusted components. In the testing, however, it is not possible to simply model the program – it is necessary instead to test the real thing (or major elements of it) under a variety of conditions – say, with carefully chosen input parameters. In most cases, this can give a degree of confidence, but there are very many (basically true) stories of software disasters resulting from an insufficiently wide range of test values having been chosen. [Ould 1990] is an excellent source for such discussions.

13. For example, during the debugging phase of a complex, highly secure operating system, a software engineer added a test module that recorded and stored the user name, plaintext password and operations performed by each and every user; the system was then shipped and installed with this debug program still in place. Fortunately the oversight was detected (accidentally) before the hole could be discovered and exploited.

14. Complex systems are usually constructed from 'building block' components that have been proved reliable in the past; these might be implemented as *objects* for example. Despite the assumed reliability, in secure systems it is normal to retest these basic blocks, and to test the system repeatedly as the blocks are combined to produce the final system. This is known as 'integration' testing, and is essential as the complex systems are gradually produced. However, the security of the system depends upon *all* of the components being adequately tested in a 'free-standing' form, and all possible combinations of conditions being tested as the components are integrated. The sheer complexity of modern systems makes this all but impossible for all but the simplest of cases. Where a secure system must also do useful work (the most usual situation) this can mean that the system is simply too intricate to allow all each and every one of the millions upon millions of relationships to be assessed.

15. Popper, for example, argued that science advances not through proving theories *true*, but rather by proving inadequate theories *false*. As each theory is swept away, it is replaced by a similarly transient new idea – which can never be demonstrated categorically correct, but is merely able to withstand the attack of counter experiments. Since the next experiment may prove it to be wrong, no theory should ever be held as more than a temporary and convenient description of nature.

16. These classes run from D1 (which represents no security measures at all), to A1 (which represents a so-called 'verified design'). The different categories indicate the different types of security measure and systems in place. DOS, which provides no identification or separation of users, is of D1 grade. A well managed UNIX machine, in which users assign file access permissions carefully, would probably gain a C1 certificate – but extensions to the basic UNIX mechanism, as in IBM's AIX for example, can give a C2 system. At grade C2, the operating system carefully discriminates between users, and most importantly it runs a continuous 'Audit Log' to track and assign responsibility for every action relevant to security – ie, accessing key files, changing permissions, etc. For the majority of applications, even C2 (running time-consuming logging processes) is sometimes thought excessive. For military or highly sensitive applications, the B grades (B1 to B3) provide even more security, with a small set of trusted programs and data structures (the 'Trusted Computer Base', TCB) having been rigorously tested and proved. Although the *full* system can never be proved, smaller and easily isolated sections such as the TCB can, but this

is very difficult in practice. The current most secure operating systems are at B3 level – in which the TCB acts as a monitor for *all* activities. Finally, A1 represents a B3 system for which the implementation, shipment and installation have all been rigorously assessed; no system meets this criteria. While the categories show the things that the system has implemented – that *should* provide high levels of security – they are no guarantee that the system will remain secure during its operation and as new hacking attacks are developed [Garfinkel 1996, Tanenbaum 1992 and Malik 1996].

17. This in fact is one of the most worrying elements within system security. When somebody leaves an organisation, it typically takes several weeks (sometimes even months) for their account and password to be changed. More worrying still, *colleagues* of the person seldom, if ever, think to change their passwords. At least in some cases, these leavers might then be motivated to break into the system – having previously learnt the available passwords. Good system security starts with good password management.

18. In 'standard' UNIX these permissions cover *read* and *write*; for files that contain programs, the permissions also include *execute*; and finally, for directories, the permissions include *search*. Three categories of users are then recognised. Firstly, the owner of the file. Secondly, every user is a member of so-called 'groups' of users – perhaps associated with a project or category of users (students, staff and admin, for example); permissions can also be assigned to other members of the user's group. And finally, global permissions for all other users can be assigned. With this, the owner of a file can establish permissions so that only they can *read*, *write* or *execute* the program; members of the group can *read* or *execute* it; but any other users are unable to do either [Tanenbaum 1992]. With the Access Control Lists discussed below, this is extended so that a specific, named user – not necessarily a member of the file owner's group – can be given specific permissions [Garfinkel 1996]. A final point to note with file permissions is that in all cases, the user with identification number zero (the 'super-user' or *root* user) is unconstrained by any of these access protection mechanisms – hence, hackers usually seek means whereby they can masquerade as the super-user.

19. Firewalls are specially designed servers through which all Internet traffic must flow before it enters a company's private, internal network of systems. The advanced security protections on these systems are designed to restrict the type of traffic and commands – and even users – that are allowed through. They can also limit

the Internet sites to which a company's staff can connect, allowing control of illicit site access [Garfinkel 1996].

20. In time, the majority of crimes could involve a computer element – as cars are increasingly protected by computerised alarms and immobilisers; as buildings are protected by computerised locks; as computerised smart cards replace wallets, tickets and identification documents.

21. Through bribery or (more worryingly) increasingly now at the point of a gun. This has become *big* business for the thieves involved: lorries carrying components have been hijacked by armed gangs, and even whole warehouses have been systematically emptied. Not all such attacks have been untroubled, however: in a recent robbery in London, the thieves entered an anonymous office block via scaffolding erected along the back wall. During the robbery, the thieves were interrupted by a passing employee, who was told that they were performing normal 'maintenance' duties. Unfortunately, when the thieves finally left, hold-alls overflowing, they discovered that the 'anonymous office block' was in fact a police station, and the passer-by a plainclothes detective! They were caught, redhanded and redfaced, and arrested.

22. The UK police's estimate for the cost of such crimes is £200 million; however, once the cost of lost business, time and market confidence is included, the cost can be multiplied by at least a factor of five [Warren 1996]. In the US the situation is even worse: estimates suggest losses of $8 billion in 1995; and Silicon Valley companies are losing $1 million worth of chips per *week*! [Lawrence 1996].

23. My favourite such guess is that the value of the metals used within catalytic converters on modern cars will soon be appreciated by the criminals – just as the value of lead roofing on churches was recognised – leading to an equally endemic spread of thefts of these components, a theft that requires roughly the same low levels of technical skill and high levels of opportunism as chip theft.

24. These figures were published in [NCC 1996]. The report was sponsored by NCC, ICL and the UK ITSEC organisation. A questionnaire was sent to some 9500 UK organisations – but only 661 responded! The absolute numbers were also very low: the three per cent figure quoted in the text represents just 33 incidents of 'external access'. In addition, there were several other breaches that may well be seen as 'hacking': 21 'line taps'; 65 illicit internal access breaches; 156 instances of staff computer misuse; and 491 of user error. Some or all of these might represent abortive hacking attempts.

25. [Warren 1996] suggests that less than five per cent of firms whose computers had been hacked even realised it; and a Pentagon report illustrates this further, with only four per cent of hacking attacks being detected at all. But yet the numbers are certainly growing rapidly – [Warren 1996] also quotes US figures, showing a rise in hacking from 132 in 1990, to a staggering 195 *per month* in 1994.

26. CERT (Computer Emergency Response Team) for instance was established at Carnegie-Mellon University in the aftermath of the Internet Worm (discussed below) to coordinate global efforts at controlling any subsequent security breaches. In 1994, for example, they issued 122 advisories – and the numbers have continued to rise throughout 1995 and 1996; the CERT Web site is now one of the largest collections of reported security breaches within the Internet, reporting some 3000 in 1995.

27. This is a fairly recent security weakness, involving the manner in which Kerberos permission tokens are generated by a pseudo-random number. Analysis has shown that these numbers can, under limited circumstances, be predicted – allowing hackers to confuse or circumvent the software system issuing permissions to access protected files. While this does indeed require careful analysis, other recent breaches require little or none – for example, recent releases of some UNIX implementations had a poor implementation of the remote login program, that allowed users to *force* an unchecked login for any valid user name – including that of root!

28. In the Prestel case (discussed in Chapter 4) the hackers were able to access the system having discovered the administrator's password pinned to a notice-board in the Prestel machine room!

29. This of course played a central role in Clifford Stoll's detection and pursuit of hacking spies in the 1980s, brilliantly described in his classic *Cuckoo's Egg* [Stoll 1991]. Such auditing is in fact an essential element in the detection of any form of digital crime, as Chapter 5 discusses.

30. One infamous hacker is Kevin Mitnick – the author of the 'Sequence Attack' described below – who is alleged to have caused over $80 million worth of damage through his hacking activities and is currently facing over 100 years in jail!

31. Many of the banks saw an interesting element of this criminal penetration of computer systems by their users. Banking staff would try to defraud the bank of money, sometimes by manipulating the computer system. However, within the banks, computer security *and* banking procedure security provide protection. Some of the insider attempts were made by those who knew how to manipulate the computer, but not the banking audit procedures

that would be affected; others could manipulate the procedures, but not the computers. In the early days, therefore, such manipulation by bank staff would be easily detected, and could usually be uncovered by security staff through simply interviewing likely candidates. As computer skills develop, however, it becomes more likely that computer expert banking professionals will be able successfully to defraud accounts.

32. My own introduction to 'hacking' came through this issue of disk space allocation. On smaller systems, it is necessary to limit the amount of file space (measured in 512-byte 'blocks') per person. As a young student, my allocation was 50 blocks. In time, of course, I wanted more – so naturally I began to seek a way to increase the allocation. Inevitably – by examining 'shell scripts' that performed administrative tasks – I stumbled over a simple trick to get 'root' privilege, thereby increasing the allocation to 100 blocks – an alteration that was immediately noticed by the system administrators! Of course, some time later, I discovered that I could solve the problem without recourse to such underhand tricks. Instead of altering *my* allocation, I changed the ownership of the file I wished to save, assigning it to one of the administrators who had unlimited numbers of disk blocks. I made the file readable and writeable by anyone (and therefore myself), but stored it in a directory to which only I had access. It didn't count against my allocation, but only I could use it – and the administration staff never caught on. Moral: it is not always necessary to subvert logical security in order to subvert the *purpose* of that security.

33. There is some confusion – and indeed contention – as to the appropriate term. 'Hackers' in the UNIX context are expert system users. Conversely, 'Crackers' are those who seek to use their expertise to break security systems. In the early 1980s, however, the print media popularised the term 'Hacker' to cover *both* types – or used the UNIX alternative 'Guru' for experts. To avoid confusion, we will use the word 'Hacker' to mean those who try to break into systems, using their expertise for illicit – or at least, mischievous – purposes.

34. Interestingly, this self-same justification was presented by the Nobel-winning physicist Richard Feynman for his safe-cracking and lock-picking exploits during World War II and the Manhattan Project [Feynman 1985]. Also interestingly, Feynman uncovered many security holes in those combination locks, the equivalent to loopholes *still* exploited by hackers today: combinations based on birthdays, on mathematical constants, etc; the equivalent of

modern passwords based on surnames, car registration numbers and so forth.

35. This is not, of course, limited to UNIX. Many universities also used the DEC VAX systems, running VMS. Although this was more carefully constructed than the initial UNIX systems, it too had security failings – including most notoriously fixed login names for system engineers, along with (widely known) default passwords: an open door to the student hackers!

36. This analogy is perhaps more apposite that it first appears. Hackers, particularly the young, attempt to break security with the same attitude as computer game players demonstrate: single mindedness; enjoyment in the intellectual challenge – but much, much more importantly, a belief (more, a solid *conviction*) that the security hole exists, just like the way to resolve a particular problem in a computer game like Zork actually exists. It is this mental attitude – much more than the technical skill – that is important in a hacker, and which must be understood by those who would seek to stop them. It is also this attitude that security project teams seek to introduce when they include a (hopefully reformed) hacker as part of the team.

37. Bruce Sterling gives a particularly interesting study of the hacker mentality and the reaction it produced in the US authorities responsible for their pursuit and capture [Sterling 1992].

38. To quote Thomas Jefferson, 'he who lights his taper at mine receives light without darkening me.' He was writing, of course, before the birth of a global, multi-billion pound printing industry had been established!

39. The Information Security Breaches Survey [NCC 1996] mentioned above quotes the maximum reported cost of unauthorised external access as just £50 000 – a surprisingly low value given the amount of damage a hacker *could* cause (*cf* note 30 on Kevin Mitnick). However, the maximum cost in the other categories was £750 000 for theft – which could also have involved hacking activity.

40. In spoofing, a hacker would write a program to mimic the appearance and action of the log on program itself. It would ask for the user's name and password, but would then store this in a separate, secret file. The poor user would simply believe that he or she had initially typed the password incorrectly, While the spoof program had in fact collected and stored the valid password for later use by the hacker [Stoll 1991, Malik 1996, Garfinkel 1996]. Modern day versions of this simple trick appear widely within the Internet – where users are invited to provide a password to secure authenticated access to certain sites. Many unwitting Internet users,

however, type the *same* password that they have on their system (to save on remembering many different passwords). The spoof involves collecting these, together with the address of the system and the user's name, and then breaking security there. In other real-world cases, even autobanks have been spoofed, with criminals installing fake ATM and then simply collecting the cashcards that innocent passers-by try to use!

41. Perhaps the most famous such gang, however, was in Germany: the 'Chaos Computer Club'; mainly comprising students and ex-students in their late teens or early twenties. Where the US and other gangs undertook most of their activities for fun – or at least, out of curiosity – the Chaos gang was far more nihilistic, deliberately causing damage on a large number of system, or stealing data to be sold for the cash used to feed drug habits: digital low-life of the worst kind.

42. For example, some of the simplest early breaches involved poorly written system utilities that, for instance, didn't check to ensure that programs run by the utility were indeed the intended program. These utilities would run as 'set user id root': that is, when they ran, it was as though they were being run by the system administrator (the 'root' or so-called 'super-user') of the system. Such users within UNIX, VMS, etc are unrestricted in the type and nature of system access they allow. A super-user can delete any files, change system monitoring details, and completely hide within the operating system. In fact, one of the earliest such breaches I personally learnt to use was within UNIX utilities that called further programs, but which did not check the names of these programs too closely. By fooling the utility into ignoring the '/' character (used for separating directory names from file names), I could have it run a local program called 'bin', rather than a system program '/bin/adduser'. By providing a copy of the 'shell' (the UNIX command interpreter) I then had unrestricted, root-privileged system access. Such individual weaknesses within system components were, however, systematically repaired throughout the 1980s, so that now only the most abstruse of holes remain. (See [Stoll 1991] for an alternative but similarly simple operating system breach.)

43. This is, of course, a very simplified description of the Sequence Attack process, which relied on the construction of locking packets generated from an unused Internet address, so that they could not be acknowledged. It also relied upon the characteristics of trust between the two systems, particularly, that the victim could be persuaded that a root user from a third (the hacker) system was

the root user from the trusted system – this attack would only work for those hackers who have previously acquired root status on some other system. Because at least some of the communication has to come explicitly from the hacker's own system – so as to ensure that sample packets are available to determine the sequence number (the packet's unique identifier) by examining the pseudo random number generator characteristics – this means that the hacker must break security at the remote site, so as to prevent back-tracing. A more complete description is in [Malik 1996].

44. Shimomura and a US reporter specialising in the hacking scene, John Markoff, wrote a brilliant book describing the search for the culprit: *Takedown* [Shimomura 1996]. After a great deal of effort, they tracked the attack back to Kevin Mitnick, a well known hacker who has already served a one year sentence for hacking. At the time of writing this, Mitnick is in a Los Angeles jail, and it is alleged that he is responsible for some $80 million of damage to computer systems.

45. A forty bit long key can give 2^{40} possible combinations of keys. This is a very large number – about one million millions – but it is not *impossibly* large for a computer. Estimates suggest, for example, that 120 Pentium PCs could break a 40 bit key in just eight days. This, in fact, was one of the successful attempts against the Netscape scheme run by a group of French schoolchildren using a smaller network of Intel Pentium processors at their school. A longer key inevitably makes a brute force attack not impossible, but definitely impractical for all those without the resources of a supercomputer network – such as the US National Security Agency.

46. Indeed, at the time of writing, Microsoft and other US companies are under increasing pressure from European computer manufacturers and software vendors to provide means whereby increased levels of security can be provided to their customers. While the banks enjoy the use of their own proprietary and highly secure encryption systems for intercommunication, messages from their account holders and accessible to hackers are a problem that could seriously hinder the development of a true Cybernation economy. In the US, Senator Patrick Leahy introduced the Encrypted Communications Privacy bill earlier this year in an attempt to address this problem. The proposed bill has the backing of, amongst others, Bob Dole.

47. As discussed above, many Internet sites post urgent notices drawing attention to the existence of security loopholes, and also providing fixes or recommendations. COAST, CERT and many university

sites provide this service. Not all system administrators, however, take advantage of this – and as Chapter 6 describes, the 'front-line' of the Information War will be those commercial organisations that are insufficiently secure.

48. SATAN (Security Analysis Tool for Auditing Networks), for example, which runs a series of security probes, attempting to identify the use of common passwords or the presence of other weaknesses that might have been corrected elsewhere. This posts notification of the weaknesses back to its operator. Originally written to help system administrators identify weaknesses in their *own* systems, it has become increasingly popular with the hackers.

49. And this of course is helped by the widespread availability of inexpensive but inordinately powerful computers – even to the home PC market. A top-end, Pentium-based desktop machine, with huge disk and memory capacity, is far more powerful than even the fastest of machines when UNIX, VMS and the rest were first developed.

50. Consider, for example, the likely result of locking out known system administrators!

51. Notice, this is different from the related tactic of 'fingerprinting' source code with unique aspects – perhaps even harmless but deliberate 'errors' – to allow the authorship of the program to be established in the event of a dispute. This will be addressed in a later chapter.

52. Many early programs were written to store the date in only two character locations, ie, '72' instead of '1972'. Date calculations are therefore performed by comparison with just the last two characters of the year, instead of the full four. As the year changes from 1999 to 2000, these calculations will yield strange results as subtractions are performed against '00' instead of '2000' – thus, a person born in 1962 will have an age calculated as '00 – 62', or '–62', instead of '2000 – 1962'. Depending on the application, this will give quite bizarre results – an expectation that is leading to a feeding frenzy within the computer industry to address and correct the untold billions of lines of code that might be affected. The widespread expectation is that the new millennium will be met by an inestimable number of computer failures associated with this 'feature' of older programs. Once the prospect of 'Millennium Viruses' has been added to this concern, it gives rise to the potential for even greater problems.

53. [NCC 1996] shows that the maximum reported cost of a single virus incident was £100 000.

54. Robert Morris Jnr is in fact the son of the famous Bob Morris,

author of the UNIX password program and Chief Scientist at the computer security arm of the US National Security Agency.

55. The 'shell' program is the UNIX process that reads users' commands from the keyboard and attempts to execute them; a 'remote shell' is therefore just such a command interpreter, but running over a network connection rather than to a locally connected terminal.

56. The most interesting such breach relied on a common programming mistake in almost all UNIX programs – that can in fact be traced to the original C Programming Manual examples. Characters input to a particular program are usually copied into a fixed size buffer *without* checking to see whether or not the size of the allocated storage space has been exceeded. Some of the UNIX programs which are available to remote systems suffered from this weakness. The Worm exploited this by providing a program on the target system with sufficiently many input characters to overflow the input buffer. Once the buffer had be filled, the input characters then overwrote parts of the program's private memory – with code to copy and execute the Worm program locally – and then overwrote the 'return address' for the program. As a result, the program was persuaded to run the Worm's code instead of its own! [Tanenbaum 1991, Malik 1996, Garfinkel 1996, Stoll 1991] This error – or oversight – has been corrected on most UNIX systems, although it is of course possible that there may be other programs that can be similarly subverted.

57. They are also now being integrated with other applications, particularly via Microsoft's ActiveX facilities, to allow distributed applications to be delivered (to PCs or the simpler 'Network Computers') over the general Internet, or over company-private 'Intranets'. This allows a centrally managed, widely distributed application environment to be implemented and supported within the Internet protocols, extending the usefulness of the Internet beyond the initial examples.

58. There are a number of research projects active within the US and the UK, examining the threat and the potential of such hostile applets; these projects (for example, at Princeton [Dean 1996]) frequently publish reviews within the Internet, but sensibly limit their discussion of the specific security breaches that they find and exploit. Notwithstanding this 'self censoring', there are other Internet publishers – such as DigiCrime – who revel in more detailed disclosures of these aspects. Because of this disclosure, it is safe to assume that such hostile applets will spread rapidly and became an increasingly widespread element of future Internet-enabled crimes.

59. It is easy to conceive of such 'fooling' applets that ask a long series of questions of the user, the answer in every case being 'Yes'. Amongst the questions, however, could be buried a request to access an external file – and lulled by the previous questions, the user will unwittingly allow this more threatening action. It will not work in *all* cases – but it will surely work in *some*.

60. A recurring theme in discussions about Internet and the law is the difficulty of defining laws and regulations that can be applied to such a pan-national institution. It is often wrongly assumed that because of the difficulty of enforcing the laws, they do not apply! This is categorically incorrect: obscenity, fraud, copyright and many other legal protections *all* apply within the Internet – although it may in practice be difficult to prosecute criminals outside of the UK, EU or other judicial areas.

61. PGP is a widespread encryption tool that can be used to protect e-mail or sensitive files – it is public domain and freely available from very many sites on the World-Wide Web. Its author, Phil Zimmerman, was threatened with prosecution by the US government for the illegal export of 'munitions', but this case has now been dropped. SET, by contrast, is an 'official' encryption tool produced by VISA and Mastercard to secure credit card transactions over the Internet. American Express and Microsoft have both agreed to use the standard, although some banks have argued that it is cumbersome to apply. Together with an extended version of Netscape's SSL, PGP and SET are likely to provide the basic foundations of secure communications within the Internet.

62. These uses of technology are interesting in their own right, quite apart from the possibility of application by criminals. There is, however, nothing new in such uses: during the Second World War, for example, a scheme for communicating with allied spies was developed – although it was not widely applied. In this, two separate and distinct radio channels were used, each individually being entirely innocent. If combined – by placing two radios a fixed distance apart – a disembodied voice from the midpoint could be heard, delivering the appropriate message. This is the audio version of the now popular 3D images, which at first glance appear to be merely scrambled dots (and which could also be used within the Web!).

63. These and other similar tricks for hiding illicit or private material without recourse to encryption are described in a recent book [Wayner 1996]. This is called 'Steganography'.

64. The reader interested in such error correction and detection algorithms is advised to consult [Halsall 1996, Tanenbaum 1989] or

a similar textbook. The subject is fascinating and technically demanding – and leads naturally to discussion of the techniques as applied within satellites, radio telescopes and a host of interesting areas.

65. The question is reasonably straightforward: are you buying an instance of a specific, real-world 'thing' (such as a picture), or merely something that will perform a task (a 'service') on your behalf?

66. Please note – this is *not* intended to be a definitive statement of the way in which HM Customs & Excise would use the relevant laws, nor of the ways in which a court would decide in the event of any dispute. Instead, this is meant simply to illustrate the type of complicated issue that should be considered in this apparently simple situation.

67. This is only possible if the so-called 'Symbol Table' has been included as part of the compiled code – a practice that is common when the program is being developed and tested; but it is usual for this information to be discarded when the software is made generally available.

68. For example, telephone fraud (the origin of the word 'phoney') is still a growing and vibrant illegal economy. It is helped further by the carefully collected databases described in Chapter 1. Con-men can obtain detailed lists of telephone owners, and arrange to pull out only those who are, for example, elderly and disabled; these can then be targeted in cynical attempts to fool them into paying for non-existent or unwanted services. This draws fewer headlines than Internet credit card fraud, but is still the most worrying (and unfortunately, *lucrative*) aspect of information age crime.

69. This last has become a growing worry in the Internet, with a mounting list of cases in the US and UK. However, these seldom go to court, but rather are settled by the payment of money [Lockett 1996]. An interesting recent situation in the UK might pave the way for stricter controls of the use of company names – and even trademarks – by non-owners. In anticipation of the merger of Glaxo and Wellcome, the name Glaxo Wellcome was registered and then offered for sale to the merged company. The judgement in the ensuing case was that such a registeration was unfair. While this did not involve the Internet *per se*, it is clear that the finding could be applied in practice. At the time of writing, Harrods themselves (who already have 'harrods.co.uk') are seeking to transfer the domain 'harrods.com' from the current registrant. Many other cases are proceeding in the US (see [Lockett 1996] for further details of these).

70. Of course, since the credit card companies' advice is not to provide card numbers and other details over the Internet until such time as secure encryption technologies are in place – specifically (in the case of VISA, Mastercard and American Express) the SET mechanism – this protection might well in fact be absent.

71. In 'caching', data that is retrieved is stored locally – this is so that subsequent requests to access the data can be satisfied locally (and much faster) without the need to re-retrieve the data. This simple mechanism can dramatically improve system performance, although it can lead to problems where the data is changing rapidly, and the cached version is therefore soon out of date.

72. And of course, while one might carefully check one's own ISP and even the trader, it is all but impossible to discover the identity of the *trader's* ISP – and this too is a place at which fraud or abuse can occur [Lockett 1996].

73. Having said that, the Mafia *et al.* have a growing interest in many other elements of digital crime – and even a stake now in chip theft. The Russian 'mafia'-style gangs have a worryingly strong grip on the country's inter-bank computer network, and the various Asian criminal gangs have entered credit card fraud and software piracy in a big way.

74. Of course, in the case of the major drug producing countries of Central and South America, these transactions *are* the economy of a small country – or rather, that economy represents a subset of the drug money laundering.

75. And there are a lot of such transfers. The UK clearing system between banks in the UK, for example, moves around £100 billion per day! Although secured by sophisticated encryption and protection mechanisms, this makes a very attractive target for criminals.

76. A survey by Booz-Allen & Hamilton banking consultancy found that in August 1996, 154 European banks had established an Internet presence, although most were little more than glorified brochures. However, a quarter of these sites are providing a set of banking transaction services equivalent to telephone or even high-street facilities. The survey found that the cost to establish such sites was around the $1m mark – versus just $25 000 for the simpler Web versions – but that the cost of an average transaction was just 13 cents – compared to a cost of 108 cents for a 'high-street' branch. The survey also produced interesting forecasts, suggesting that the number of Internet banks would rise rapidly from the 1996 figure to some 2000 by the end of the decade.

77. A feat attempted (or at least, detected) some 250 000 times in 1995, and thought to have been successful in the majority of cases!

78. It was this question of 'permanently depriving' the rightful owner that led the UK authorities to establishing specific regulation against so-called 'Joyriders'. In this case, the car is 'borrowed' simply to allow the driver to play with it – once satisfied, the car is abandoned, to be returned to its owner. Because the intention is always to return the car, straightforward theft is not appropriate, and so the 'taking and driving away' without consent element had to be added to the law – an example of responsive legislation-making in the event of societal changes.

79. This chapter draws on three specific texts. For the US legal situation, I have used [Cavazos 1994], and for the UK [CCTA 1996] and [Smith 1996] – along with [Lockett 1996]. In addition, the EFF archives within the Internet ('www.eff.org') provide a wealth of detail on specific situations.

80. This directive covers the ways in which member states interact with one another in the enforcement of regulations covering activity that crosses borders. It is not intended to cover the regulation of Internet-related activity *within* the member states' own jurisdiction. Many observers (myself included) would dearly like to see a more comprehensive application of this philosophy of regulation applied throughout the Internet-accessible world, allowing 'data havens' gradually to be eroded – and allowing a more sensible, global policing of the Cybernation to be effected.

81. Usenet news articles are disseminated rapidly and automatically by protocols that run continuously on all Internet-connected hosts. To filter the newsgroup articles – of which there are many thousands produced hourly – at any single host would be a job of Herculean proportions; for this reason, ISPs are encouraged (by the Home Office in the UK, for example) to exercise control at the point of *production*. Even this, however, is fraught with difficulty.

82. These denial of service attacks represent in many cases *spiteful* hacking attempts. E-mail bombing involves the transmission of very many, very large files of garbage to a particular computer – the result is to effectively block the legitimate use of the computer's e-mail facilities. This attack was most famously used to punish the earliest attempt at Internet advertising by two US lawyers [Barrett 1996a]. Autodialler attacks involve repeated login attempts that either target known user identities (thereby preventing them from logging in legitimately) or simply seek to lock out particular terminal or modem lines by blocking them.

83. It is perhaps better even than the alternative model for computer hacking, which centres on analogies with *trespass*. However, as every bar-room lawyer knows, 'trespass' must involve the *intent to damage* once access is gained. Since hacking most usually is performed with a view to copying or accessing information – involving no such damage – the analogy is at best only a loose one.

84. The precise wording: '. . . making a false instrument, namely a device on or in which information is recorded or stored by electronic means with the intention of using it to induce the Prestel computer to accept it as genuine and by reason of so accepting it to do an act to the prejudice of British Telecommunications plc.'

85. In fact, there is a close relationship in principle between computer and 'real-world' frauds – with many possible analogies. For example, a recent UK case uncovered a loophole in the regulation of firearm certificates. To buy a gun, it is necessary not only to hold such a certificate but also to show it to the person from whom the gun is to be bought. Certificates must be authorised by the Chief Police Officer of the city or county within which the buyer lives. A convicted criminal was, however, able to buy a gun through mail order – and unfortunately then use that gun to murder an innocent woman for no readily apparent reason. The murderer obtained the certificate by himself advertising a gun for sale, and receiving an valid certificate from a prospective buyer – this is the certificate he used to authenticate himself in his own mail order purchase. The analogy with computerised permission tokens in multi-computer networks is obvious – by 'advertising' non-existent services requiring access permission tokens, a hacker can obtain and then use such a token in secure communication with a third party. This type of subterfuge is therefore important both in fraud and in computer hacking.

86. Because the computer crimes are defined in the context of *fraud*, the laws come within the US Treasury department – specifically, the purview of the US Secret Service as the investigative arm of the Treasury. One of the most secretive and protective of US organisations (responsible also for the close protection of the US President) has therefore been given responsibility for investigating and pursuing hackers, who are perhaps the individuals with most interest in publicising information that others would wish to hide. For example, a US hacker called Ed Cummings published a picture of a Secret Service agent picking his nose! Quite separately, Cummings was arrested in March 1995 and charged with various hacking-related offences on the basis of his possession of phreaking

devices and illicit information such as passwords. In May 1996, he was fined $3000 and sentenced to two years' imprisonment. Within the hacking community, it is claimed that the Secret Service targeted Cummings deliberately because of his publication of the uncomplimentary picture – there is, of course, nothing to suggest that such an interpretation is at all valid, and there is no doubt that Cummings was indeed a hacker.

87. There are some differences between Scottish and English law in many regards, but not in the case of computer misuse or related aspects.

88. My own, simplistic first venture into the world of 'computer hacking' (mentioned above) would therefore now be seen as an arrestable, criminal offence – resulting, potentially at least, in a fine, imprisonment and a criminal record. In practice, as we shall see, most 'victims' are unwilling to bring such prosecutions – but this would still have been sufficient to have dissuaded me from the attempt!

89. After six years, by August 1996 there had been only some forty prosecutions under the UK act. Interestingly, the first attempted prosecution under the UK act came in 1993. This was of an alleged hacker, Paul Bedworth – who was acquitted on the equally novel defence that he was addicted to the activity!

90. Beyond this, however, as Chapter 5 discusses, many companies also have only low levels of confidence in the police's ability to handle such crimes – and also fear the seizure of their equipment and operational data for use as evidence.

91. Despite the overt clarity of the laws, there are still a number of criticisms that can be laid against them from a legal perspective – for example, the Computer Misuse Act does not define many of the key terms that are relevant to it, such as 'computer' or 'program'. While this might be seen by non-lawyers as a ludicrous objection, based on the splitting of hairs, it is nonetheless an important failing.

92. One might also recommend that companies avoid this situation by posting clear messages on login screens indicating that access to the computer is covered by the employees' terms and conditions – particularly with regard to exceeding authorisation in access rights. While this message would not stop such accesses, it would make it clear that the access was in contravention of the employment terms, although whether this would have any power in the case of already dismissed employees is a moot point. In [NCC 1996] only 17 per cent of organisations had such a display of system access rights on or near the terminal, and less than half

of the organisations had any form of publication of these access rights in terms of documents or similar distributed to their staff.

93. The Constitution forms the highest legal authority within the United States. To ensure that it became a 'living document', able to respond to specific situations, the framers allowed a mechanism whereby further 'Amendments' could be added – thereby extending the Constitution's scope. The first ten such amendments, covering items central to the *individual* rather than the *nation*, are the 'Bill of Rights'. The history of the emergence of the US itself – in protest against intrusive, absentee government on the part of Great Britain – particularly sensitised the framers of the Constitution to the influence of government on the individual. The Bill of Rights was therefore conceived with the definite intention of protecting citizens from government intrusion, providing such aspects as protection of the privacy of mail, of worship, and from the billeting of soldiers on one's land. See [Brogan 1985] for a more detailed discussion.

94. The US have also the 1980 'Privacy Protection Act', which was created to protect *publishers* from the intrusion and seizure of material by government investigators – other than in the case when the publisher was the immediate object of a particular investigation [Cavazos 1994]. This and the ECPA were important elements in the 1993 ruling against the US Secret Service in the case of 'Steve Jackson Games' – considered in Chapter 5.

95. These eight principles state that the personal data must be: obtained and processed fairly and lawfully; held only for the lawful purposes described in the data user's register entry; used and disclosed only in the ways described in their entry; relevant for the purposes described; accurately maintained; held only for as long as necessary; available for correction by the individual to whom it relates; and securely protected [DPR 1996].

96. That is, the individual must be informed of the fact and the purpose of the data collection, in such a way as to allow them to judge whether or not such collection and subsequent data use is in their interests. If the data is being collected for provision to another company, for example to support direct mailing of advertising, the person concerned must be informed of this quite explicitly. They must also be provided with the opportunity to walk away from such collection processes, or to object to the proposed use.

97. Hence, of course, the famous 'Man on the Clapham Omnibus' in the trial of *Lady Chatterley's Lover*.

98. This observation is more important than it might at first seem to be. The Internet is a wholly new medium: it is neither a print

medium nor a broadcast medium; it is a little of each, but not *exactly* like either one. Many of the arguments about Internet obscenity (and defammation, etc) hinge on this point. The ISPs and others (such as in the case against the Communications Decency Act, addressed below) would wish to use the 'print' model – with its defences for 'common carriers', innocent publishers, etc. By contrast, the so-called 'Moral Majority' have proposed that the model be taken from the TV medium – with regard to aspects such as nudity and bad language accessible to minors. In passing we might remark that, as a wholly new medium, an approach based on an Internet-specific model (rather than a clumsy development of pre-existing models) might well prove to be more successful.

99. For example, in the UK the Metropolitan police have written to UK ISPs requesting that certain newsgroups featuring child sex, etc should be withdrawn. While both the police and the Home Office have stressed that they have no wish to enforce regulation, it is clear that the expectation is that ISPs will have to carry responsibility for what they 'print' or 'broadcast'.

100. Consider, for example, if it were known that a public figure – a politician, say – was having an affair, and that it was known exactly which hotel, room and so forth they were using. Although a blackmailer might be unable to obtain a true photograph of the couple making love, a computer-generated image could easily be produced – using the exact room, and morphed images of the people involved. When presented with the 'photograph' – and assuming it was of a plausible scene – the politician might well subject to the extortion attempt involved. This will be seen as an important aspect of 'disinformation' campaigns in the Cyberwar context in Chapter 6.

101. These two cases are: New York v. Ferber 1982; and Osborne v. Ohio 1990 respectively [Cavazos 1994].

102. Although at the time of writing there have yet to be any attempts to apply such regulation in practice.

103. A recent UK case of criminal damage (carried out against a warplane) would seem, however, perhaps to give a possible defence in this and related cases: those who damaged the warplane did so, they said, to prevent a worse crime (the bombing of innocent people in the country to which the warplane had been sold) – they were acquitted. The vigilantes in the paedophile revenge situation might well be able to claim a similar defence – although the analogy is far from perfect, and it is unlikely that any court would want to establish such a precedent, even assuming that the vigilantes could be found and prosecuted.

104. The police in the UK have already, for example, gained success in retrieving stolen items and prosecuting burglars by the simple expedient of establishing their own jeweller's shop, performing fencing activities from a back room. In this case, the police secretly filmed and recorded the visitors to the fence and then later used the tape as evidence. The analogous Internet situation is easily imagined.

105. Although, it must be admitted, these and other judicial IT systems – such as the CRAMS system for the Probation Service, and MASS for the Magistrates Courts – have seemingly all suffered from delays, cost over-runs and management problems. The total IT spend by UK police forces, for example, is expected to be a massive £200 million in 1996.

106. 'Trawling' involves an investigator – say, a tax officer – examining a vast collection of related records (perhaps of all individuals working as taxi drivers in a given city) with a view to finding fraudulent returns. Where there is a reason to support such wide-scale investigations, they *can* be carried out – but the inspector would have to have more than idle curiosity to justify it. There would have to be very good *a priori* evidence to suggest that more than an individual taxi driver was potentially guilty of an offence. For this reason, investigators cannot simply make huge collections of all available information on every citizen, and then perform automatic searches looking for evidence of wrong-doing – the protection of civil liberties, the Data Protection Act, and of Parliament makes this impossible.

107. This involves finding those items which refer to the same person – even though the names might be misspelled (deliberately or accidentally). In the UK, for example, such data matching between social security, benefits agency and tax record databases would allow a clear understanding of benefits fraudsters to be derived – and such data matching exercises are an active and interesting area for the government, given an estimated cost of £5 billion for such frauds (see, for example, *Computing*, 23 May 1996, p. 8).

108. An early implementation of such expert systems – called Eliza – was so convincing that many users would quite happily tell the program their deepest, most personal fears and concerns, even knowing that it was nothing more than a program [Rich 1983].

109. A prototype for this screening exercise has been developed and was tested throughout 1995 and 1996 by the UK's Inland Revenue. Similar implementations have been produced in Denmark and elsewhere, including a system used by the UK's Customs and Excise.

110. Triage is a medical process. Victims of an accident – or a battle – are divided into three sets for attention: those that do not require urgent attention, and that can therefore be put to one side for the time being; those that are so badly hurt that they will definitely die, and must therefore be made comfortable through painkillers; and finally, those that will benefit from urgent and immediate attention. This apparently cold-blooded approach to such emergencies is, on many occasions, the only realistic tactic.

111. An alternative to these is called 'genetic' algorithms. In this, a set of defining characteristics for an algorithm are determined in advance – although it is not possible to know exactly what values should be used. Genetic algorithms work by choosing a set of values at random and repeatedly running the algorithm with these values. The 'success' of the algorithm is recorded, and a small subset of moderately successful values are retained. These, in the form of a 'DNA string', are then combined – as though through mating – and the algorithm again run. By retaining only those sets of values that are the most successful, over a repeated series of experiments, the algorithm will gradually converge on the optimum values. Unlike neuron nets or expert systems, this method relies on the programmer already knowing the *type* of algorithm required, even if not the values to be used – it is only therefore applied in a restricted set of circumstances.

112. In a fascinating – and even worrying – experiment in Japan, an artificial 'baby' has been produced in a neuron net [Rossney 1995]. This baby demands attention from the computer user, and tries a series of childlike tactics to attract the user. It cries, shouts, smiles and gurgles; if ignored, it 'remembers' the most successful tactics and repeats these until 'rewarded'. Interestingly, if subject to abuse – such as repeated ignoring or inconsistency on the part of the user – the baby becomes increasingly irrational and withdrawn, mimicking in many ways the actual behaviour of real babies. This is a disturbing program to observe – but shows that while artificial *intelligence* is difficult to produce, artificial but human-like *behaviour* is easier.

113. Or rather, it would learn to *duplicate* the results of the inspectors, but we would have to assume that they were 'correct' and thereby provided the base for assessment.

114. For example, *Computing*, 23 May 1996 reported UK Stock Exchange plans to use just such systems (along with so-called 'Fuzzy Logic' reasoning) to track fraudulent dealing – although the development of the system was seen more in the context of *prevention* than of detecting such cheating.

115. The Pentagon, for example, have claimed that less than five per cent of security breaches are detected at all! [Warren 1996].

116. In UNIX, a file is deleted in a two-step process. Firstly, the entry in the directory within which the file was held is altered. The file's name is not removed, but the means of accessing the file *is*. Secondly, the data blocks on the disk are detached from the ex-file's 'header' – again, so that they cannot be accessed. As more files are then created, the blocks and the directory entries will be overwritten, but they can be expected to remain in place for some little time – and therefore to be accessible to the suitably expert technician.

117. Indeed, [Garfinkel 1996 p. 785] recommends *not* involving police officers unless 'real loss' has occurred – ie, the security breach has resulted in theft or caused costed damage. In some cases, the resulting 'downtime' from seized equipment can in fact destroy a business.

118. And of course, elsewhere throughout the world. The Canadians, French, German, Dutch and Australian authorities are all working hard to counter not only the hacker threat, but also this low appreciation of their abilities.

119. The UK 'Starburst' inquiry, for example, was handled by the West Midlands Police in Birmingham, simply because it was first alerted to a Birmingham-based paedophile. Thereafter, the inquiry has covered most UK cities – moving well beyond the 'normal' jurisdiction of the Birmingham officers involved.

120. This is of course a gross simplification of the E911 debacle. [Sterling 1992] provides significantly more detail, together with a valuable and insightful discussion of the motives of the several organisations and individuals involved.

121. Under certain circumstances – such as to protect an informant, for example – the *text* of a search warrant need not be shown to the subject of the search. In this case, only the warrant's existence is communicated to the suspect.

122. In response to the cyberspace civil rights abuses that apparently resulted from the 'hacker crackdown', Mitch Kapor (founder of Lotus) established the EFF as an active campaigner in support of Constitutional protection for cyberspace activities. In June 1996, for example, the EFF was instrumental in the successful challenge to the Communications Decency Act.

123. However, the judge did not accept that the seizure of the BBS counted as 'interception', but rather 'unauthorised disclosure' – a condition for such interception was that it be 'contemporaneous with its transmission'. This means that such interception is more

closely akin to seizing documents than to deliberately overhearing on-going communications [Cavazos 1994].

124. See [Barrett 1996b] – this discusses the technical and legal situation of such evidence in more detail.

125. In the criminal case, this is a simpler condition to satisfy: the police can show, for example, that although the system *had* been penetrated – and was perhaps not therefore 'working properly' – the hacker was unable to modify the audit log, which therefore was not affected by the improper operation; it can therefore be entered as evidence.

126. Unfortunately, as Lord Woolf himself notes in his interim report – Chapter 13, para. 11 – the technology provided is already of insufficient power to support the case load management, word-processing, e-mail and text retrieval applications envisaged.

127. See, for example, [Susskind 1996] for more detailed examples of the possibilities inherent in technology within courts and the legal profession in general.

128. Just such a 'walk through' and VR model was used, for instance, in the recent US trial of O. J. Simpson – although it was considered to have been a 'gimmick' rather than a useful explanatory tool.

129 This boastful attitude on the part of the hacker is attested to by many of the police or other investigators that pursue them. A society whose actions are all too often illicit and hidden, it is as though the bright light of official attention makes them *want* to justify – and thereby explain – their actions; some even look to teach the police how the hacker activities actually work! A further example of the essential immaturity of the majority of hackers.

130. Described in the *Daily Telegraph*, Monday 18 December 1995, 'War of the Microchips'. The officer involved launched the hacker attack using loopholes in the MILNET electronic mail system, that allows programs to be executed in a remote and privileged manner. To the ship's system, the information appeared to be an innocuous text file, but the message fooled the e-mail system into copying and executing a carefully constructed set of instructions – allowing the officer super-user status within the system. Although this would have soon been noticed, he was then able to disarm the system's audit defences – leaving him in control of the core command system, and hence of the ship. The precise details of the attack have remained a military secret, although many in the hacker community have been able to describe the likely mechanism in detail.

131. Both quotes from 'War of the Microchips'.
132. 'Hacker war' is a straightforward aspect of Cyberwar, involving simply the offensive hacking activities – but performed for and on behalf of the government. Thus, a 'military hacker' (there is as yet no name for such a specialist) would penetrate and damage an enemy's computer system just like a home-grown, civilian digital vandal would seek to exploit or damage a bank's (or even a government department's!) computer.
133. Or sometimes C³I war – for Command, Control, Communication and Information systems warfare.
134. *Sunday Times*, 4 August 1996. 'American spies hack into Euro computers to steal trade secrets', by Tim Kelsey and David Leppard. An unlikely story, claiming that the CIA in particular had not only accessed the EC computers, but also those of the Japanese and French governments. In part, this can be considered unrealistic given the conflict between the CIA and the NSA over whose responsibility such an illicit, electronic information gathering activity would be – and given the likely damage-to-benefit ratio that such an exercise would imply. Nonetheless, the activity itself *would* be eminently possible – even it was unlikely to have been attempted by the US government against its allies.
135. For a fuller, detailed and excellently told account of these problems – and of the legal clampdown on phreakers and hackers that followed – [Sterling 1992] is highly recommended.
136. Perhaps the earliest such, and the one in which the term 'Cyberwar' was introduced, is the now classic [Arquilla 1993]. This was followed by a flurry of papers through 1994 and 1995, summarised in [Waller 1995].
137. In many cases of Elint it is not necessary actually to read or understand the content of a message – so that decryption becomes only a minor part. Instead, intelligence about the *fact* of a particular type of broadcast can be as important. For example, a particular level of radio traffic, of a certain sort, can allow an eavesdropper to deduce the presence of a Brigade headquarters – and by triangulation, deduce its location.
138. Notwithstanding this, some recent reports [Richardson 1996] have suggested that France in particular are developing military vehicles equipped with the necessary equipment to perform such monitoring; this has, however, never been confirmed.
139. Other than in the case of the Pearl Harbour attack. But arguably, this wasn't so much a case of 'fighting' as of being 'ambushed' – and Pearl Harbour itself would probably be thought of as being outside the national sanctuary anyway.

140. For example, sympathisers could be incited by the introduction of material within Internet newsgroups. This could introduce false and malicious information in a 'non-official' way, to an audience already suspicious of its own government's information sources. In passing, however, we might remark that the government itself could also make use of these newsgroups, to introduce its own counter-information: a war of words, waged within cyberspace!

141. By contrast, the UK has a more vivid memory of fighting within the homeland – from the Blitz to Irish terrorism. This is perhaps why the US has reacted so strongly and firmly to the Cyberwar potential, while the UK (although equally recognising the *threat*) has been significantly more relaxed. In the US, such vulnerability has come as a rude awakening; in the UK and throughout Europe, related terrorist outrages such as disinformation campaigns and soft-target bombing have come to be accepted as part and parcel of modern life – the threat of hacking attacks in place of mail bombs is perhaps even welcomed as a 'softer' alternative!

142. That having been said, such alleged Cyberwar tactics were claimed to have been enacted by BA against Virgin Atlantic as part of the improbable 'dirty tricks' campaign.

143. Not all such intellectual – rather than political or ideological – protest groups would be seen as 'middle class terrorists': there are certainly intelligent, articulate protesters who would never descend to violence. Nonetheless, there is a definite group of educated, university-graduate protest groups that have resorted to a variety of unsavoury tactics: the firebombing of laboratories or even of experimenters on animals are perhaps the most obvious. Many might share the emotional aspect of the protesters' concerns; few would sympathise with their methods. These groups include, however, a growing number of people familiar or even expert with computers – simply because the total number of such people within the overall population is growing. It is inconceivable that such computer-literate, protest-motivated individuals will not think to use hacking, virus or other Cyberwarfare tactics as part of their activities. Should the use of such tactics rather than firebombs be applauded? This is a complex, moral maze into which I would prefer not to tread!

Index